Education
and
Political Independence
in Africa
AND OTHER ESSAYS

Education
and
Political Independence
in Africa

AND OTHER ESSAYS

L. J. LEWIS

*Professor of Education and Head of the Department of
Education in Tropical Areas, University of London
Institute of Education*

GREENWOOD PRESS, PUBLISHERS
WESTPORT, CONNECTICUT

Library of Congress Cataloging in Publication Data

Lewis, Leonard John.
    Education and political independence in Africa.

    Reprint of the ed. published by Nelson, Edinburgh.
    1. Education--Africa--Addresses, essays, lectures.
I. Title.
[LA1503.7.L48 1973]   370'.96   73-7380
ISBN 0-8371-6929-1

Originally published in 1962
by Thomas Nelson and Sons Ltd, Edinburgh

Reprinted with the permission
of Thomas Nelson & Sons Limited

First Greenwood Reprinting 1973

Library of Congress Catalogue Card Number 73-7380

ISBN 0-8371-6929-1

Printed in the United States of America

Contents

	Acknowledgments	vi
	Introduction	vii
1	Education and Political Independence in Africa	1
2	Higher Education in the Oversea Territories 1948–58	13
3	Anglo-American University Co-operation in the Changing World	39
4	Partnership in Oversea Education	64
5	The British Contribution to Education in Africa	80
6	Education and Social Growth	96
7	Social and Cultural Problems of Urbanisation for the Individual and the Family	113

Acknowledgments

Permission to reprint these lectures has been given by various journals and institutions. The following list gives full details, and the author and publishers wish to thank all concerned for their co-operation.

EDUCATION AND POLITICAL INDEPENDENCE IN AFRICA   Read at Barchembeweging, Vereniging Woodbrookers, Holland, 3 August 1960

HIGHER EDUCATION IN THE OVERSEA TERRITORIES 1948–1958   Reprinted from the *British Journal of Educational Studies*, Vol. VIII, No. 1, November 1959, by permission of the Editor of the *British Journal of Educational Studies* and Faber and Faber, Ltd., London

ANGLO-AMERICAN UNIVERSITY CO-OPERATION IN THE CHANGING WORLD Section of a work paper prepared in conjunction with Professor Karl W. Bigelow, Teachers' College, Columbia University, April 1960, for the use of the *Committee on the University and World affairs*, created by the Ford Foundation, 1959; reprinted by permission of the Ford Foundation

PARTNERSHIP IN OVERSEA EDUCATION   An inaugural lecture delivered at the University of London Institute of Education, 5 February 1959; reprinted by permission of the University of London Institute of Education and Evans Brothers Ltd, London

THE BRITISH CONTRIBUTION TO EDUCATION IN AFRICA   Read to the Commonwealth Section, the Royal Society of Arts, 8 November 1960, and reprinted by permission of the Society

EDUCATION AND SOCIAL GROWTH   An open lecture delivered at the University College of the Gold Coast, 12 November 1956, and reprinted by permission of the University of Ghana

SOCIAL AND CULTURAL PROBLEMS OF URBANISATION FOR THE INDIVIDUAL AND THE FAMILY   Read to the Tenth Anniversary Conference of the Institute of Rural Life at Home and Overseas, 11 May 1960, and reprinted by permission of the Institute

The publishers also wish to thank the following for their kind permission to use the photographs of which they hold the copyright as part of the cover design : Central Office of Information ; Tanganyika Information Services ; Ghana Information Services Department ; Punjab Photo Service.

Introduction

The recent political changes in Africa and Asia have focused attention on and aroused concern for education especially in those countries now assuming political responsibility for their own affairs. Much of the concern is emotional in origin rather than based upon a knowledge of the facts about what has been done or about what remains to be done. The decision to print in one volume this selection of papers, previously presented to limited audiences interested in education in oversea territories, was made in the belief that the information they contain and the views expressed would throw some light on contemporary discussions among those concerned about the progress of education in Africa and Asia. In making the material available to a wider audience it is hoped that opinion on education in Africa may be better informed and less emotionally conditioned.

The first paper, *Education and Political Independence in Africa*, was prepared for a study group organised by the Dutch branch of the Society of Friends which met at Barchembeweging, Vereniging Woodbrookers, Holland in August 1960. In it the influence of the policies pursued by the colonial powers is touched upon, the magnitude of the task that faces the newly independent countries in trying to expand their education systems is examined, problems of the content of the curriculum at various levels are discussed and the possibilities of international co-operation are referred to briefly.

The second paper reviews the British contribution to the development of *Higher Education in the Oversea Territories 1948–58*, focusing attention upon the progress made and some of the problems that have arisen. This review has particular relevance to the plans for expansion of university education envisaged in East and West Africa. It has bearing too upon the significance of the increasing participation by the United States in higher education in the newly independent countries.

The problems of co-operation between persons and institutions of differing traditions is examined more closely in the paper on *Anglo-American University Co-operation in the Changing World.* Given here is that section of the paper prepared by the author as a British contribution to an Anglo-American study.

The subject of Anglo-American co-operation in the furtherance of education in Africa is dealt with in *Partnership in Oversea Education,* an inaugural lecture delivered at the University of London Institute of Education in 1959. It serves to emphasise the fact that there already exists a body of knowledge based upon experience, on which to build for the future.

The paper that follows, *The British Contribution to Education in Africa,* read to an audience of the Royal Society of Arts, provides a summary review of the growth of education in British Africa and emphasises the continuing importance of the policies that were developed during the past half-century. One of the lessons to be learned from this experience is that education is fundamental to the social, economic and political well-being of a community. Aspects of this are dealt with in the last two papers reprinted here. In the lecture *Education and Social Growth,* delivered at the University College of the Gold Coast, the subject is examined with reference to the contribution that a university institution can make to the teaching profession through research and through co-operation with official and voluntary agencies concerned with education. In the paper on *Social and Cultural Problems of Urbanisation for the Individual and the Family,* read at the tenth anniversary conference of the Institute of Rural Life at Home and Overseas, the problems of urbanisation of traditional rural societies are examined. This is a process that has just begun for many of the peoples outside Europe and is occurring at tremendous speed. Constructive adjustment to the changes will be dependent to a considerable extent upon the development of education to fit the changing conditions.

L. J. L.

I

Education and Political Independence
in Africa

' It is no use rushing matters or pretending that political decisions are an adequate substitute for planning and partnership for education and economic development.' *The Times*, Saturday, 6 June 1960.

In the article from which the above quotation is taken the writer draws comparison between how independence was achieved in Ghana and in the Belgian Congo. It is used here because it summarises the relation between education and political development that forms the thesis of this paper.

The first point I wish to make is that whilst there is a close relationship between educational policy and the development of political independence, this does not necessarily mean that one particular educational policy is necessarily the only right one, whatever right may mean in this context. The educational policies followed in the past in Africa by the major colonial powers have differed considerably in character. Any attempt at comparing the educational policies of different countries involves generalisation, a process always open to misunderstanding and distortion. Even so it is necessary to attempt, briefly, to generalise about the policies pursued in the past by Belgium, France and Great Britain.

The French assumed that French civilisation was the best of all possible civilisations, saw the French mission in Asia and Africa as bringing other people in, and visualised France Metropolitan and France d'Outre Mer as a unity. In educational terms this was interpreted in Africans and Asians learning to be French. Education was planned, on the one hand, to provide for the vocational needs in relation to the requirements of agriculture, trade, industry and administration, and, on the other hand, to ensure that the necessary élite should be truly French.

Belgian policy was much more parental in concept and assumed a long period of tutelage, during which the attainment of material well-being was the first priority. In consequence, the provision of educational facilities omitted serious consideration of anything other than vocational needs, and these related mainly to subordinate responsibilities.

British policy, less logically thought out than the others, from the 1920s onwards, was governed by the assumption that political independence was a foreseeable endpoint; at the same time it was much influenced by economic and social considerations.

If these generalisations are valid, it follows that British policy would be the one most likely to have prepared the Africans for political independence. But the best that can be said about it is that political independence has come more smoothly to British West Africa than elsewhere. Whether this will continue to be so is open to question. If some of the newly independent French territories are in difficulties, and this is certainly true of the Cameroons and of the Congo Republic, equally is it true that some of them, Male, Sudan, for example, are coping well with their immediate problems. However, it can be said with a reasonable degree of authority, that whatever the educational policy pursued, those territories that have longest enjoyed an educational system which attempts to provide education at all levels, are most likely to survive the hazards of assuming political, economic and social responsibilities consequent upon political independence.

Having indulged in that degree of generalisation let us examine the state of education in various parts of Africa. Now, whether a government has come early or late, to recognise that political independence is the goal of its African peoples, it is accepted that democratic independence, in the Western sense, necessitates intelligent participation by the mass of the people in the running of public affairs at local, national and international levels. This is not possible without an educated franchise. The

2

acceptance of this premise has resulted in attempts everywhere to provide a minimum of basic education for every child, and to intensify efforts to achieve adult literacy.

The approach has varied. In Ghana, Western and Eastern Nigeria the attainment of universal, free primary education has been made an absolute priority. In other English-speaking territories under British control this aim has been accepted as the long-term plan. In French-speaking Africa too the principle is accepted, each region being allowed to work out its own rate of progress.

Consequent upon this policy there has been, in every instance, a phase of rapid expansion. This has strained the resources in respect of the provision of buildings and equipment, has resulted in serious dilution of the teaching profession and has reduced the effectiveness of supervision. Even where no attempt has been made on political grounds to provide free primary education, most African communities have shown so intense a desire for education for their children that governments have been forced to step up the rate of expansion. Between 1946 and 1956 school enrolment in most territories expanded over 100 %. In one group of territories (in the former French Equatorial Africa) the increase in enrolment was 314·5 %. In the Western Region of Nigeria, where a system of free and universal primary education was set up in 1955, the increase in the primary school enrolments was 142 % in five years. In Ghana the primary school enrolment rose from 154,360 in 1951 to 455,053 in 1958.

In every case the political decision to expand primary education was taken because governments realised that only an informed electorate can exercise political responsibility, and that the implementation of plans for social and economic development is dependent upon the intelligent co-operation of the community and an adequate supply of skilled manpower.

It is less easy to determine where the credit lies for the decisions made and for the response obtained. Whilst it is true to say that the climate of political opinion contributed to the acceleration of the rate of expansion of primary education, it must be recognised that expansion was being planned before the full significance of the nature of the political developments had become clear. Equally difficult is it to determine to what extent local politicians stimulated the demand for education by giving it priority in their policy statements for their electioneering campaigns, or to what extent they were giving explicit expression to the desire of the people. Apart from these political pressures, it should be remembered that the foundations for the expansion of primary education that took place in the late forties and fifties had been laid by missions and government effort in the previous quarter of a century.

The rapid expansion of primary education has created a number of problems of great moment. The numbers of teachers required rose far beyond the resources available for training them. The number of pupils able to move on to secondary schools had always exceeded the number of places available ; as primary provision expanded so did the pressure on the secondary schools, at a time when financial resources had been strained to their limits. Because of the intense parental interest in schooling, there has been a general lowering of the age of admission, with the result that large numbers of children exhaust the provision of formal education too early to enter upon gainful employment, even when such opportunities offer.

But before considering these problems, it would be wise to get some measure of the provision at present available. In doing so it must be recognised that some of the data is not reliable. In the introductory remarks to the provisional report *On the Needs of Tropical Africa in the Field of Primary and Secondary Education* [1] it had to be recorded that ' Of the twenty-two countries and territories covered by the inquiry, only eleven had replied to the questionnaire at the time the Secretariat began summarising the results of its study '. Furthermore, the method of presentation of data is far from satisfactory. Indeed, so unsatisfactory is the present state of affairs that two of the four objectives given to the delegates of the Unesco Regional Conference on the International Standardisation of Educational Statistics at Khartoum in 1959 were : ' To clarify certain ideas

[1] Unesco/Ed./Africa/2 Paris, 15 January 1960

4

on how to realise a strict international standardisation of educational statistics ', and ' To make different countries aware of the importance of educational statistics in planning the economic and social development of Africa '.

With such reservations as are implied in these remarks in mind, the picture presented to us in twenty-two territories is as follows [1] :

Territory	School Age Population *	Year	Primary School Enrolment
Central and West Africa			
Belgian Congo	2,711,800	1957/58	1,572,824
Cameroons (French)	640,000	1958	293,977
Ivory Coast	618,000	1958	125,727
Dahomey	345,000	1959	81,107
Gabon	82,000	1958	39,763
Gambia	58,000	1958	6,465
Ghana	967,200	1958	540,921
Upper Volta	694,000	1959	40,923
Liberia	250,000	1959	53,232
Nigeria			
Lagos	67,400	1957	56,688
Northern Region	3,608,600	1957	205,769
Western Region	1,347,200	1957	982,755
Eastern Region	1,585,400	1957	1,209,167
Republic of the Congo	156,000	1958	78,962
Senegal	460,000	1958	80,473
Sierra Leone	428,000	1958	69,276
Soudan	740,000	1958	42,052
Togoland	220,000	1959	78,689
East Africa			
Ethiopia	4,000,000	1958/59	158,005
Federation of Rhodesia and Nyasaland			
Northern Rhodesia	444,000	1958	243,926
Nyasaland	520,000	1958	269,693
Kenya	1,198,000	1958	601,410
Madagascar	1,010,000	1959	364,217
Uganda	1,153,000	1957	418,179
Somaliland (Italian)	264,000	1958/59	16,485
Tanganyika	1,733,067	1958	403,301

* Estimated at 20 % of the total population

[1] Figures supplied by Unesco/Ed./Africa/2 Paris, 15 January 1960

Excluding the Lagos figures, as representing an arbitrary unit within a territory, the highest ratios of enrolment are Eastern Region, Nigeria, approximately 80 % ; Ghana, approximately 60 % [1] ; Belgian Congo, approximately 55 % ; and Nyasaland, approximately 50 %. By contrast the Northern Region of Nigeria has approximately only 5 % of the children of school age attending the primary school and former Italian Somaliland approximately 6 %.

Now the significance of these figures, despite the tremendous expansion that has taken place, is that, except for a few isolated areas, such as Lagos and the Northern Rhodesia industrial area, every country is still faced with a formidable task in providing primary education for every child of school age. The task is seen to be all the more formidable when it is recognised that facilities for the training of teachers must be improved in quality and greatly expanded in quantity.

In all countries there is a lack of teachers to fill the new posts, and in most countries, except at the lowest level of the unqualified and untrained teacher, there are additional difficulties that arise from wastage. Indicative of the dimension of the problem is the situation in the Northern Region of Nigeria, where pressure for expansion is still low, and where only one child in eighteen of school age is enrolled in the primary school : each year five hundred teachers or 5 % of the total primary teaching staff needs to be replaced. Only in Ghana and in Northern Rhodesia can it be said that the supply of teachers for primary schools is beginning to approximate to needs in terms of satisfactory minimum qualifications and numbers.

Apart from any questions of policy in respect of the recruitment and conditions of service of teachers, changing political conditions have exercised a profound influence on the status and the attractiveness of the teaching service. Where steps have been taken to prepare for political independence, teachers have been in great demand as persons with suitable educational

[1] Sample analysis of the recent census returns suggest that the number of children of school age has been seriously under-estimated. Strenuous attempts to bring this up to 100 % are being made.

6

qualifications to serve on committees as elected or nominated representatives, to take the lead in political organisations and to accept membership of parliamentary and local political machinery. In consequence the schools have suffered on two counts. At all levels of political activity it has meant a considerable degree of absenteeism from school duties ; in addition the more able or the more politically active members of the profession have left the profession for full-time public or political service. This, however, is not the whole story. Political independence is invariably accompanied by an expansion of public services, the development of diplomatic services and the deliberate reduction in the number of expatriate officers. The teaching profession, as the main pool of educated persons, is drawn upon by government, commerce and industry to meet their more immediate needs.

The response of governments to the losses thus suffered by the teaching service have been disappointing. Various stop-gap measures have been attempted, such as temporarily lowering the standards of academic and professional qualification and easing the conditions of training. What has not been seriously attempted is a reassessment of the whole process of the provision of education in terms of the current social and economic conditions. The primary school curriculum is still in all essentials that portion of the traditional curriculum that can be encompassed in the four or the six years of compulsory schooling, devised essentially to lead on to the conventional secondary school. Some attempts have been made to relate the primary curriculum to the rural conditions in which the majority of the pupils live. But for the most part the work in the primary schools is dominated by the interests of the small number of pupils who will have the benefit of further secondary education. How few these are is made clear by the following analysis of the provision of secondary school places available. In Ghana, where provision is relatively generous, only 15·4 % of the primary school enrolment can go on to secondary schools. In six of the countries listed in the previous table the proportion of secondary school to primary school places is between 5 % and 10 %, and in six of the other

7

countries the proportion is limited to 1 % of the primary school enrolment.

These figures show clearly that the vast majority of children can expect nothing more than a minimum period of formal education, in most cases four to six years. Yet they will have to match up to immense political, economic and social responsibilities in conditions of great strain. The failure to give adequate recognition to this fact means that teacher training too is looked on in anachronistic terms ; and its improvement and expansion is seen as a task beyond the financial resources of most territories in the foreseeable future. Another outcome of this is the reluctance on the part of governments, except that of Ghana, to accept responsibility for improving teachers' salaries, with the result that the social status of the teaching profession is falling at a time when education is generally recognised as the keystone to development.

Whatever assistance for expanding education may be provided from outside sources it will be necessary to re-examine the content of the curriculum and the methods of training the teachers. Alternatives to the traditional pattern of schools must also be sought if some of the more urgent needs are to be met in the foreseeable future. At the same time methods of effective political education of the community will have to be devised. Here the newly independent governments have failed as completely as did their predecessors, despite the existence of official information offices. In Ghana the middle school leaving examination had to be resuscitated because the community had not been prepared for the idea of dispensing with it. Failure to prepare the people for increased local rates to meet the costs of universal free primary education had equally unfortunate consequences. In the Western and Eastern Regions of Nigeria there were similar failures.

If the people are to accept their personal responsibility for providing education and to co-operate with the government they must know the facts about the changes and developments necessary and understand their importance to the future well-being of the community. This is a lesson that is not yet fully appreciated by many of the political leaders. It is a lesson that must be learnt if genuine local responsibility is to be developed.

Turning to secondary education and to technical and vocational education at the secondary level, the enrolment figures for the countries previously referred to are as follows :

Territory	School Age Population *	Year	Secondary Enrolment	Technical and Vocational Enrolment
Central and West Africa				
Belgian Congo	2,711,800	1957/58	12,158	28,677
Cameroons (French)	640,000	1958	6,645	3,344
Ivory Coast	618,000	1958	4,310	794
Dahomey	345,000	1959	2,881	737
Gabon	82,000	1958	1,025	131
Gambia	58,400	1958	674	47
Ghana	967,200	1958	83,096	4,979
Upper Volta	694,000	1959	1,841	502
Liberia	250,000	1959	3,046	592
Nigeria				
Lagos	67,400	1958	4,591	1,578
Northern Region	3,608,600	1957	3,651	872
Western Region	1,347,200	1957	46,810	220
Eastern Region	1,585,400	1957	12,242	3,100
Republic of the Congo	156,000	1958	1,975	1,284
Senegal	460,000	1958	5,066	1,036
Sierra Leone	428,000	1958	5,904	333
Soudan	740,000	1958	1,790	959
Togoland	220,000	1959	1,847	526
East Africa				
Ethiopia	4,000,000	1958/59	4,496	2,450
Federation of Rhodesia and Nyasaland				
Northern Rhodesia	444,000	1958	1,890	1,840
Nyasaland	520,000	1958	1,169	927
Kenya	1,198,000	1958	3,922	1,114
Madagascar	1,010,000	1959	19,116	6,314
Uganda	1,153,400	1957	21,599	3,807
Somaliland (Italian)	264,000	1958/59	822	915
Tanganyika	1,733,067	1958	3,499	1,366

* Estimated at 20 % of the total population

Now whether the estimate provided by Professor Arthur Lewis (formerly of Manchester University and now Principal of the University College of the West Indies), of the proportion of the population that should receive secondary education (4 % of each generation) in order to meet the needs for educated manpower, is accepted or not, it is clear from the enrolment figures above that the existing provision for secondary education is everywhere inadequate. If the secondary school enrolment were to be raised to 10 % of the primary school enrolment, then places would have to be found for the following additional numbers of pupils in those territories that fall short of that percentage :

Belgian Congo	145,124	Senegal	2,981
Cameroons (French)	22,753	Sierra Leone	1,024
Ivory Coast	8,263	Soudan	2,415
Dahomey	5,230	Togoland	6,022
Gabon	2,951	Ethiopia	11,305
Upper Volta	2,251	Northern Rhodesia	22,503
Liberia	2,277	Nyasaland	25,800
Nigeria		Kenya	56,219
Lagos	1,078	Madagascar	17,306
Northern Region	16,926	Uganda	20,219
Western Region	51,466	Somaliland (Italian)	827
Eastern Region	108,675	Tanganyika	36,831
Republic of the Congo	5,921		

Until the greater part of the needs indicated by these figures is met it will not be possible to expand post-secondary and university education in order to feed the professions.

The supply of teachers with adequate qualifications for secondary school teaching is still less satisfactory than is that for primary school teaching. Even in Ghana, ten years after setting up an Institute of Education to provide for the professional training of graduates, the number of candidates put forward for the first post-graduate professional examination was only 15.

Here the political leaders are faced with another problem. For prestige reasons, as well as for less emotional ones, it is necessary to recruit local graduates as quickly as possible into the administration and into the diplomatic services. Similarly, to a lesser but still significant degree, commerce and industry are anxious to obtain the services of local graduates. If these demands for qualified persons are to receive priority of attention it can only be at the expense of the secondary schools and colleges. This is a difficulty that can be met, to some extent, by recruiting expatriates. There are not the political objections, at least not to the same degree, to employing expatriates for teaching as there are for employing them in administrative posts. Unfortunately it has become increasingly difficult to recruit expatriates because contract appointments provide little security, and few opportunities for advancement. In some former British territories these difficulties have been recognised and some people sought a solution through the establishment of a Commonwealth Education Service. The failure to set up such a service when it was mooted at the Commonwealth Education Conference in Oxford in 1959 was a disappointment to many countries.

For reasons of national prestige many newly independent countries are reluctant to seek official help from the former imperial power in dealing with educational problems, yet the fact that the local education systems are closely patterned upon those of the former ruling powers makes it difficult to accept assistance from elsewhere. Some countries are now trying to meet their staffing requirements through the aid of international organisations. But recruitment through international agencies presents many difficulties and up to the present time there has been little evidence of imagination or leadership in the use of such resources.

Returning for the moment to secondary education, it is interesting to note that contrary to what one would have expected the content of the curriculum has received little attention on the attainment of independence. In every former British territory most of the secondary schools have continued to follow the English grammar school curriculum. Technical and modern curricula have received hardly any attention. In Ghana the only new feature has been the addition of French to the secondary school curriculum, but this was a direct political decision, reflecting the ' island ' nature of Ghana in relation to the French-speaking territories around it. In the French-speaking territories themselves, political independence has not produced any radical changes in the curriculum. The desire to attain full expression of the ' African personality ' has led to attempts to adjust the balance between French and African languages in education. But these attempts are inhibited by the realisation that for the time being French must continue to be the medium of instruction until there is a satisfactory supply of materials in the African languages for use in the schools. Decisions about the choice of language, both as a medium of instruction and as part of the content of the curriculum at both the primary and secondary levels, are bedevilled with political considerations. Whatever the merits of an African language, political independence tends to increase the number of international contacts and activities, which together with technological development require the use of one or other of the major Western languages. Undue educational emphasis upon the use of the mother tongue can become a decisive influence in territories where no one language or language group is dominant. Furthermore, it is difficult to arrive at right decisions about such matters as which dialect should be adopted and which form of orthography should be used, because of the lack of local linguistic specialists to advise the politicians. One of the chief defects in the newly established university institutions is the failure up to the present to develop vigorous faculties and departments for the study of African language.

The development of vocational secondary education has been more marked under French and Belgian auspices than under British. This in part reflects the differences in general policy; in part, the differences in the organisation of primary and secondary education. One factor that may alter this picture is the changing emphasis upon the value of the technician as opposed to the white-collar worker, an inevitable concomitant of economic development. This is especially true where development is planned on the basis of manpower surveys that emphasise the value of the technician and technologist. The most potent influences in this respect are likely to be the World Bank (the International Bank for Reconstruction and Development), the International Monetary Fund, the A.I.D. and the United Nations Special Fund. The objects of the latter agency are (i) to assist in making surveys of material resources and (ii) to encourage research programmes.

2

Higher Education in the Oversea Territories
1948–58

In August 1943 a Royal Commission was appointed : ' To consider the principles which should guide the promotion of higher education, learning and research and the development of universities in the Colonies ; and to explore the means whereby universities and other appropriate bodies in the United Kingdom may be able to co-operate with institutions of higher education in the Colonies in order to give effect to these principles.' [1] Two months earlier a Royal Commission had been appointed : ' To report on the organisation and facilities of the existing centres of higher education in British West Africa, and to make recommendations regarding future university development in that area.' [2] In January 1944 a West Indies Committee of the Commission on Higher Education in the Colonies was appointed : ' To review existing facilities for higher education in the British Colonies in the Caribbean and to make recommendations regarding future university development for those colonies.' The reports of the three bodies were issued in June 1945.

The facilities for higher education that had been in existence up to the outbreak of World War II consisted of (a) institutions in Malta, Jerusalem, Ceylon and Hong Kong possessing all the attributes of a university including autonomy ; except for Ceylon, they were members of the Universities Bureau of the British Empire, and (b) institutions of post-secondary education, but not of university or university college status, in some cases preparing students for degree examinations. Two institutions, Fourah Bay

[1] *Report of the Commission on Higher Education in the Colonies*, Cmd. 6647, H.M.S.O., 1945
[2] *Report of the Commission on Higher Education in West Africa*, Cmd. 6655, H.M.S.O., 1945

College, Sierra Leone and Codrington College, Barbados, were affiliated colleges of the University of Durham submitting candidates for degree examinations in arts and divinity. The Commission on Higher Education interpreted the terms of reference as being primarily the establishment of principles governing the creation of universities in areas where university institutions did not exist, but expressed the hope that the recommendations might in some instances be of value to the universities already in existence. Underlying the approach of the Commission was the assumption that the development of university education was ' an inescapable corollary of any policy which aims at the achievement of colonial self-government '.[1]

The immediate purpose was assumed to be to produce men and women with the standards of public service and the capacity for leadership which progress towards self-government demands. The creation of university colleges was decided upon as the first step towards the establishment of institutions of full university status, and the specific inquiries made in the Caribbean and in British West Africa indicated that such institutions were needed immediately. In addition the Commission supported the proposals made in 1939 for the early establishment of a university in Malaya and supported a proposal that Makerere College should be developed to university status to serve East Africa.

The Commission advocated a unitary rather than a federal approach to the establishment and development of the new institutions, and was of the opinion that they should be entirely residential. It was also at pains to point out that the idea of a university implied the study of a comprehensive range of disciplines, humanistic and scientific, the provision of facilities for the study of professional subjects and service to the general life of the community through participation in adult education and extra-mural activities.

In considering the subject of staffing the Commission stressed that, because research is an essential part of the work of a university, the size and quality of the staff must be related to

[1] *Report of the Commission on Higher Education in the Colonies*, Cmd. 6647, H.M.S.O., 1945

research and to teaching needs in order to allow time for private study. The Commission pointed out the importance of service conditions in recruiting of staff from overseas and in maintaining contact with the intellectual and academic life of the university world as a whole.

In order to ensure the interest and co-operation of the home universities in the development of the new institutions it was recommended that there should be created an Inter-University Council for Higher Education representing the home universities. Autonomy of the new institutions in the sense enjoyed by the universities in Britain was regarded as essential, and detailed suggestions were made concerning the constitution of the various college bodies, such as the college council and the senate, the former to be responsible for the government and administration of the finances of each college and the latter to supervise the academic activities.

In order that the quality of the academic awards of the new institutions might command general recognition, the Commission advised that the colleges should enter into special relationship with the University of London. By such a relationship, subject to certain safeguards, students who satisfied the requirements might be awarded the degrees of that university. It was intended that the special relationship should include the joint approval of syllabuses and examination requirements with proper attention to local conditions. The Commission stipulated that degree-granting powers could be conferred on a new institution only when the staff had had sufficient experience of work of a university standard, that their conditions of work allowed for the active prosecution of research or other original work, and that a substantial number of students had completed satisfactorily the courses leading to degrees in a sufficiently wide range of subjects. It was appreciated that special provisions might be necessary by way of qualifications for admission, and that in some cases courses preliminary to degree courses would be necessary.

The Commission pointed out that substantial financial aid would have to be forthcoming from Britain, and that generous scholarship provision would be necessary not only to assist candidates for admission to first degrees but also to make it possible for some of the best products of the new institutions to pursue postgraduate studies in Great Britain or in the Dominions.

Detailed attention was paid to the planning of professional courses in medicine, agriculture, veterinary science, law, engineering and education. The special importance of rapid progress in the latter was emphasised as likely to lead to the strengthening of the secondary schools and thereby ensure a satisfactory flow of candidates for post-secondary studies.

The Commission also gave thought to the problems common to all the territories, namely the medium of instruction, and indicated the need for those members of the university staffs concerned with the training of teachers to be exceptionally well equipped to teach English and to train their students to teach it. In those areas where the mother tongue lacked the written literature to permit of its adoption as a subject for degree studies, it was advised that the function of the university institution would be to co-operate in linguistic research and to train teachers in methods applicable to the teaching of the local languages.

The West Indies Committee and the West African Commission made recommendations which in general followed these principles, with modifications, reflecting particular local needs. The members of the West African Commission disagreed seriously on certain issues and produced a majority and a minority report. The main difference occurred in respect of assessment of the likely flow and build-up of the student body, the optimistic group pressing for immediate establishment of individual colleges in the three main territories, with an initial concentration in one or other institution of certain professional and vocational courses. The less optimistic group were of the opinion that a single university institution would be more than adequate initially, and recommended that it should be established in Nigeria, with the additional provision of separate post-secondary feeder institutions in each territory.

In 1939 it had been proposed that the King Edward VII College of Medicine and Raffles College, Singapore, should be amalgamated to form a university college. When these colleges were reopened after World War II it was realised that there had been considerable developments in the thinking about university education in the colonial dependencies. In consequence of a visit by Dr R. E. Priestley (Principal and Vice-Chancellor of the University of Birmingham, and member of the Commission on Higher Education in the Colonies) to advise on problems of university development, it was generally accepted that a university college should be established without delay. As a result of a Commission appointed in January 1947 to review the position in the light of the 1945 Report of the Commission on Higher Education in the Colonies it was decided that the transitional stage of university college status was not necessary. The reasons for this decision are important and are best shown in the words of the Report :

> Malaya has had nearly four years of enemy occupation and a difficult period of rehabilitation. Out of her sufferings have come a new energy and a more emphatic realisation of the importance of university education, not merely for training students to fill the highest posts in the country, but also for giving them the qualities of leadership and disinterested public service which are necessary for the progress of her people. There is a ' divine discontent ' with things as they have been and a recognition of the contribution which a university could make towards a standard of living, a broader culture, a closer integration of the people and a greater measure of self-government. . . . It is true that a university college could make almost as great a contribution as a university : but, however complete its autonomy and however loose its relations with the University of London it would not arouse the same enthusiasm. . . . The University of Malaya would provide for the first time a common centre where varieties of race, religion and economic interest could mingle in joint endeavour. We feel convinced that if a university were created at this juncture, it would secure a firm loyalty and an enthusiastic co-operation from all sections of the people.[1]

The outcome of these various investigations of the needs of the dependent territories in respect of higher education was

[1] *University Education in Malaya*, Col. No. 229, H.M.S.O., 1948

immediate. In the second report of the Inter-University Council for Higher Education in the Colonies, issued in September 1949, the Council stated that ' the institutions of higher education in the British Colonies and the Anglo-Egyptian Sudan with which the Council is immediately concerned, in addition to the existing universities of Malta and Hong Kong, are :

In West Africa
>   University College, Ibadan, Nigeria
>   University College of the Gold Coast, near Accra

In East Africa
>   Makerere College, Kampala, Uganda

In the Anglo-Egyptian Sudan
>   Gordon Memorial College, Khartoum

In the West Indies
>   University College of the West Indies, near Kingston, Jamaica

In Malaya
>   Raffles College, Singapore
>   King Edward VII College of Medicine, Singapore ' [1]

In 1949, in accordance with the recommendations of the Carr-Saunders Commission on University Education in Malaya, the University of Malaya was created by amalgamating Raffles College with King Edward VII College of Medicine, Singapore. Professor Michael Grant, reporting in 1957 on the year's work at Khartoum, was able to say : ' The greatest event during my term of office has been the conferment upon the University College of full University status, taking effect, by Act of Parliament of the Republic of the Sudan, on 24 July 1956.' [2]

In 1955 a further addition was made to the list of university

---

[1] *Inter-University Council for Higher Education in the Colonies: Second Report, 1947–1949*, Cmd. 7801, H.M.S.O., 1949
[2] *The University of Khartoum: Report and Accounts, 1957*

institutions, with the incorporation by Royal Charter of the University College of Rhodesia and Nyasaland. The grant of the Charter was made ten years after Mr J. F. Kapnek had offered the sum of £20,000 as an initial contribution towards the founding of a university. That gift encouraged a group of Rhodesians to form an association of ' Friends of the University of Rhodesia ' to foster the idea. Their activities under the leadership of Mr L. M. N. Hodson, Q.C., eventually led to a private Bill of the Parliament of Southern Rhodesia being passed in 1952 providing for the incorporation and constitution of the university. Early in 1953 a Commission on Higher Education for Africans appointed by the Central African Council under the chairmanship of Sir Alexander Carr-Saunders recommended the establishment of a university college on an inter-racial basis. Despite some criticism the Board established by the 1952 Act accepted the recommendation, and in 1957 the first group of full-time students entered the College at the Mount Pleasant site given by the City Council of Salisbury.

Probably the simplest measure of what has been the result of the formulation of policy in 1945 and its application since that date is provided by tabulating the student figures of the institutions in 1946, or in their first year of foundation, together with the latest figures available :

Student Enrolment	1946	1954	1958
The Royal University of Malta *	299	411	208
University of Hong Kong	109	863	1,126
University of Malaya	(1949) 645	1,043	1,640
University College of the West Indies	(1948) 33	369	605
University College of Ghana	(1948) 90	349	519
University College, Ibadan, Nigeria	(1948) 224	527	1,024
University College of East Africa	130	448	823
University of Khartoum	188	582	850
University College of Rhodesia and Nyasaland		(1957) 72	124

* Admissions are made triennially

The build-up of satisfactory staff in the new colleges and universities was recognised from the beginning by the Inter-

University Council as a matter of major concern. Whilst bare enumeration of staff numbers in itself tells little, it is worth noting that despite a close adherence to standards, which particularly in the early years occasionally made it necessary for the Council to advise an institution not to fill a vacancy, by 1954 there were 919 full-time academic, library and senior administrative staff employed in the universities and colleges.

Staff Numbers	1954	1958
The Royal University of Malta	52	64 *
University of Hong Kong	130	224
University of Malaya	161	218
University College of the West Indies	101	121
University College of Ghana	142	143
University College, Ibadan, Nigeria	126	170
University College of East Africa	100	173
University College of Khartoum	107	137
University College of Rhodesia and Nyasaland	—	61

* Majority part-time appointments

In financial terms the growth of these institutions represents an investment of funds from three sources : (i) the Imperial Government has provided capital by grants from C.D. & W. Funds, made grants through the Colonial Office vote to finance the work of the Inter-University Council, and made grants to the University of London in respect of the expenses of the special relationship scheme ; (ii) the several local governments have met the recurrent costs incurred, made capital and endowment grants and subsidised students by extensive scholarship programmes ; (iii) the third source of investment has been provided by private benefactions, which have come in part from local individuals and business organisations and in part from the great philanthropic foundations such as the Nuffield, Carnegie, Rockefeller and most recently the Ford Foundation and the Leverhulme Trust. The degree of assistance so far provided, in its very generosity and diversity, presents great problems for the future, and some consideration of them might well provide a starting-point for a review of the costs of providing for the expansion of university education.

The term ' investment ' is used here, irrespective of whether the money has been spent on capital plant and equipment, research projects or recurrent expenditure. The production of trained manpower and original work is a national investment and should not be regarded, as it still is in too many circles, as a disbursement of financial resources or indulgence in cultural luxury.

One of the most frequent comments made about the new institutions is that they are ' expensive ', frequently with the implication that possibly they are even ' expensive luxuries ', and that the service they provide might have been obtained through much cheaper scholarship programmes. It is true that, looked at in terms of immediate expenditure, both capital and recurrent, the new universities are absorbing very large sums of money, and that the *per capita* cost of each product, whether it be a university graduate or a contribution to knowledge, may compare unfavourably with costs of similar products from old establishments. But such an estimate of worth ignores the value of benefactions and facilities that lies behind the current activities of the older foundations, and the hidden subsidy enjoyed by institutions in countries where the main ancillary services, power, water, transport, communications, sewage and waste disposal are amenities shared with the general public and industry and commerce. Furthermore it ignores the significance of local national aspirations both social and political, and it assumes that instructional facilities alone are important.

Whilst the rate of expenditure on the universities during the ten years under review can be fully justified this does not absolve the persons responsible for controlling the way the money is spent from careful, continuous and even imaginative review of the demands made for funds to meet recurrent and new capital costs. The expenditure on university education must be related to other demands upon the national purse. Determining the proper proportion of the national income to be spent on university education is a difficult enough task in the United Kingdom where there is fairly general realisation of its importance to the survival of the nation. Political leaders in Britain are fully cognisant of the fact that ' the dependence of the universities on the State is balanced by a dependence of the State on the universities '. Furthermore, the University Grants Committee provides a body of experience and wisdom concerning university affairs which ensures that the soundest judgment is exercised upon the validity of the claims for money put forward by the universities. In the oversea territories at the present time, it cannot be claimed that the public as a whole knows how important it is to have within the country adequate opportunity for university education, neither can it be said that the politicians fully understand the vital part the university has to play in the life of the nation. For many years to come it will not be possible to establish the exact counterparts to the University Grants Committee. In these circumstances the advice given by the Inter-University Council to the new colleges and to the governments of the countries served by them has been particularly valuable.

Two major questions are at issue here. First, will the financing of university work be as generous as in the past now that political independence has been achieved and the university colleges are acquiring university status ? Secondly, has enough experience and understanding of machinery for evaluation and consultation accrued to make it possible for a body with similar purpose to that of the University Grants Committee to function authoritatively ?

The continued contribution of the Imperial Government and the philanthropic foundations to the finance, in their different ways, is essential to their well-being and development. For the Imperial Government the questions likely to arise include : (i) assessment of the extent to which contributions should continue to the established institutions, and (ii) the extent to which assistance shall be provided for new institutions. This will involve political as well as financial considerations. The former may include examination of the policy of continuing independent contribution as opposed to that of pooling resources with other governments to provide an international fund. A somewhat similar problem faces the philanthropic foundations. The general efficiency of the way in which foundation funds are used might well be improved if joint consultation and assessment of needs and resources were developed. In connection with benefactions there is urgent need to explore local resources and, in the proper sense of the term, exploit them in order to obtain the fullest financial maximum contributions available and, more particularly, to develop partnership between individual citizens and university. Incidentally, the study of the financing of the new institutions might well offer scope for valuable research to departments of economics in the institutions themselves. The present ' national ' and popular support, readiness to accept the pioneering challenge, and the clarity of the directive provided by the Asquith Commission coincided with a period of expanding economic prosperity. This may well be followed by a period of regression, and the other factors may lessen in significance with increasing age.

The importance of the financial aspect of the future of the new institutions has been brought out in the reports of two recent visitations. Commenting on the finances of the University College of Ibadan, the delegation of the Inter-University Council which visited the College in 1957 had this to say : ' The present state of the College's finances seems to us very buoyant. . . . The device of an expendable endowment fund (standing at June 30, 1956 at £1,342,000) provides for the time being manoeuvring room within which the College can plan its development comfortably. We are apprehensive, however, about the financial situation which may arise in some ten years' time when the expendable endowment will be exhausted and when the Government will be faced with a sudden and steep increase in its liability to the College. We feel that the College's position when that situation arrives would be much stronger if the Government could see its way to make systematic further contributions to its non-expendable endowment of the College, which at present stands at £750,000.' [1]

The Commission which visited Malta in 1957 came to the

[1] *Report of a Visitation to University College, Ibadan, January 1957*, Ibadan University Press, 1957, pp. 11–12

conclusion ' that the first task is to put the main services on a much more secure and satisfactory basis than at present obtains. . . . For if certain easily discernible basic weaknesses are not remedied in the near future, the University cannot prosper and must gradually decline.' [1]

The dependence of the University upon Government for finance coupled with the changing political situation in Malta led the Commission to a consideration of the subject of autonomy, and in paragraph 5 of the report to an exposition of the relation between universities and governments. This deserves the widest circulation, because of the latent anxiety which exists in some quarters about the independence of the new institutions, and the antagonisms which have occasionally occurred between them and governments. Because it is generally accepted that he who pays the piper calls the tune, a comment offered by the Commission on the degree to which the climate of opinion towards the University may or may not affect attitudes towards the objectives of a university is of great general value. ' A university, if it be properly so called, has objectives more distant and more difficult to achieve than even the important purpose of professional education. It must seek to advance learning in the fields with which it is concerned and in general to pursue fundamental knowledge and fundamental criticism in a fashion which sets it apart from and may even at times set it, or some of its members, in opposition to the prevailing disposition of the community to which it belongs. That service calls for expenditure only partly related to currently visible needs, and for a climate of opinion which is ready to tolerate and even to respect a dissident minority.' [2]

For these reasons it would appear to be a matter of some importance that financial provision for university education be subject to review.

Closely related to finance of the new institutions is the matter of staffing. During the years under review the results of teaching, the output of research results and examination of the degree

[1] *The Royal University of Malta : Report of the Commission, July 1957*, para. 2
[2] *The Royal University of Malta : Report of the Commission, July 1957*, para. 6

of participation of university teachers in consultative and advisory activities in their respective territories reflect creditably upon those responsible for making appointments. The extent to which indigenous appointments have been possible has been controlled by concern for standards, by availability of local candidates and by the competing interests of government, commerce and industry for the services of individuals with appropriate academic qualifications. In some colleges, because of the policy of making local appointments the oversea members of staffs are seriously concerned about their own security of tenure and opportunities for advancement. There is no simple formula that will provide an easy answer to these and kindred difficulties. Nor is this aspect of the organisation of the new institutions one which can be examined locally with the degree of objectivity and understanding necessary to provide smooth working solutions. Establishing and maintaining a satisfactory balance between the local and expatriate appointment is not made easier by the high rate of turnover of expatriate staff. Furthermore, the younger oversea recruits are usually inexperienced in university administration and politics, and there is considerable diversity in their training and experience because they are recruited from all parts of the world. The increase in the proportion of indigenous to expatriate staff is a policy that must be pursued, having proper regard to standards, and should result in a considerable reduction in salary costs. But if this policy is pursued too far the consequences may prove exceedingly harmful. The time is rapidly approaching when greater emphasis should be placed upon a programme of secondment and exchange of staff between the older and the new institutions, possibly involving the formulation of a precise scheme. By this means it will be possible to ensure the professional future of the members of staff and at the same time prevent the new institutions from drifting into isolation or becoming entirely dependent upon their own alumnae for renewal of teaching and research staff.

In the teaching work of the new universities and university colleges, whilst creditable examination results have been obtained, disappointment may be expressed at the apparent lack of imagination in compiling syllabuses and in exploring teaching techniques. More seriously, it would appear that little has been done to bring indigenous cultural and environmental material into the content of university teaching and research. There has undoubtedly been a conservative tendency arising largely from anxiety to make sure that the standards attained should undoubtedly be related, and seen clearly to be related, to United Kingdom standards. But other factors have contributed to apparent tardiness in these respects, not least the necessity for research to provide material on which to base changes in content and procedure. In some fields the lack of persons qualified and experienced enough to carry out extensive study and to interpret the original material available made it impossible to start work. When suitably qualified persons have been available and financial provision has been possible, the initial work of exploring the field of study and defining the priorities for research and teaching has taken time. It is significant that the recent visitation to the University College, Ibadan, found it necessary to suggest modifications to proposals put before them for developments in the fields of language and linguistics, religion, philosophy and in the variety of themes that for convenience might be described as African studies. In the same way they found it necessary to advise more modest approaches in the fields of veterinary science and forestry. The over-all assessment of priorities in relation to the content of courses and subjects for research is likely to become of increasing importance in the years immediately ahead, and will call for co-operation from outside as social, economic and political changes exert more pressure upon the universities.

One aspect of the teaching calls for special comment. Local needs have resulted in demands for the provision of courses of a professional nature or non-degree level to meet the urgent need for teachers, administrators and social and community development workers. These demands have tended to be met very reluctantly because of the fear of being involved in sub-standard work and a loss of status. Experience has proved such fears to be ill-founded, and it would appear that, especially in such courses provided for experienced non-graduates, contributions of lasting value can be made in some fields of investigation through the students' activities, and that out of their personal maturity they contribute to the general life of the college.

The dependence of the university institutions upon an adequate flow of candidates for admission from the secondary schools has led the university teachers to participate in secondary school work in a variety of ways such as advising on the content of the curriculum, judging the adequacy of the qualifications of teachers of special subjects and giving guidance about the equipment of science laboratories. This work has been specially valuable to examining authorities for the purpose of giving recognition to schools. In addition, some university teachers have helped in school textbook production and in the in-service training of teachers to a much greater extent than is common in Britain. The greater part of this work, by United Kingdom traditions, is regarded as the responsibility of institutions of education and departments of education, and where these have been established overseas they have to a greater or lesser degree made useful contributions. They have, however, been most effective where they have been able to obtain the active co-operation of members of other faculties by contributing from their special studies to solving school problems and meeting school needs. This might appear to be an interim state of affairs, but the best experience does suggest that in the newly developing nations there is scope for developing more direct participation of university teachers generally in the work of the schools.

In the field of extra-mural studies and general extension work too, it would appear that the time has come for reassessment of the function of the new university institutions. The present extra-mural and extension work is essentially in the United Kingdom tradition. A direct result of the thoroughness with which the United Kingdom universities have discharged their responsibilities for supervising the growth of the new institutions is the tendency of these institutions to follow closely the United Kingdom pattern, despite the generous proportion of teachers drawn from other lands and participation in the work by Fulbright, Ford and other American sponsored scholars. This is a weakness and there is a strong argument particularly for a review of extra-mural extension work by a team including American and local representatives as well as persons from the United Kingdom.

One specially important problem that will need to be solved in the near future is that of defining the scope of the research work in the new institutions. Without exception the new universities and university colleges are serving communities which are involved in the early stages of political, social and economic change without possessing the facilities for the expanded programmes of applied research on the scale necessary to meet the tremendous demand to exploit local resources. The extent to which the university workers have co-operated with governments, business and industrial organisations in seeking answers to current problems has been almost entirely dependent upon personal decisions about the extent to which they should participate in the study of immediate working problems. The personal decision, especially in the case of the young recruit, is not always an easy one to make and in respect of locally recruited workers is fraught with tension as between satisfying an urgent local community need and satisfying academic interests and proper personal ambitions. Refusal to participate in a piece of applied research can be misunderstood, particularly by politicians anxious to press forward with development programmes, and could lead to clashes between the university institution and the government. A way of dealing with this problem which might be given consideration lies in the establishment of National Research Boards, the membership of which would be drawn from the political and administrative branches of government, trade and industry, and the universities and university colleges. Such bodies, established initially with consultative and advisory duties, could develop machinery to ensure the maximum contribution from the university workers whilst avoiding any infringement, directly or indirectly, of their freedom. A further advantage of such machinery is that it would contribute to breaking down the 'ivory-towered isolation' of which university personnel have been accused, sometimes with justification.

It might well appear that the encouragement of such national bodies is likely to make the university research worker more open to pressure from political and vested interest, and that such a state of affairs is likely to intensify the apparent conflict between 'pure' and 'applied' research, and to create an atmosphere incompatible with detached survey and study. Co-operation and consultation are much more likely to lead to mutual understanding than is any attempt to keep apart from such applied research. More arguable is the thesis that such national bodies are likely to be antagonistic towards the development of co-ordination of effort that has been manifest in recent years at the international level. Economic and social considerations are, however, likely to prove greater than political neo-tribalism, and the effectiveness of the work of the Commission for Technical Co-operation in Africa South of the Sahara, and of the Scientific Council for Africa South of the Sahara, has already established the concept of international co-operation. The build-up of national consultative machinery between government and industry and institutions of higher education could add considerably to the efficiency of research planning and to the use made of the results.

The insistence that all students should be in residence was made for two reasons. There is fundamental value in scholars living and working together, and for many of the students the conditions in their lodgings would be inimical to study. The residential facilities have in every case proved satisfactory, ranging as they do from hostel conditions to the completely Oxbridge collegiate type. But the intimacy of mutual scholarly life between teachers and students has by no means been fully established. In consequence, the strength of the continuing *alma mater* tradition is nowhere developing as it ought. The reasons for this failure are many, and frequently understandable if not always excusable. The language barrier is undoubtedly considerable. Cultural differences have sometimes tended to be emphasised by an exaggeration of national traits and habits on the part of students and some local members of the academic staffs. Many expatriate teachers have seen their responsibilities so completely in terms of research and teaching that they have ignored or not recognised their wider responsibilities. The aberrations of the odd expatriate characters who have indulged in whimsical or patronising adoption of local costume, food practices and other superficial forms of identification with the people of the territory have served to set apart rather than to draw together the different peoples. The problem resolves itself into two parts, both of which must be dealt with if the new institutions are to provide a satisfactory contribution to the societies they are intended to serve. On the one hand there is a need for constructive and continuous effort to bring about the brotherhood of scholarship and learning ; and on the other hand there is a need to adjust, modify and develop the character of the university institutions as part of the community. Neither of these objectives will be easy to attain, but the energy and thought expended in establishing the new universities will not have full reward until these problems are solved.

The administration and government of the new institutions have in general been formulated in terms of (i) a Council of laymen and academic persons presided over by a Chancellor, President or Chairman, exercising sovereignty and accepting ultimate responsibility, and (ii) the Senate (or equivalent body) responsible for advising on academic and financial matters. In the early stages the senior administrative officers, that is to say the Principal (or Vice-Chancellor), Registrar and Bursar, sometimes found it necessary to make decisions on policy without prior consultation with the academic body. Such decisions on occasion caused offence to the academic bodies. Different institutions have devised their own varieties of consultative machinery, drawing very much upon procedure in Britain. Such imitation cannot always be said to have proved satisfactory. The need for procedures offering adequate and fluent means of consultation between the Council, the administrative officers and the academic body will increase as the institutions grow in size and in the range of their activities. Moreover the excuse of urgency for making decisions without consultation, valid in the early stages, will no longer be justified. Review and, where necessary, prompt revision of machinery and procedures is likely to call for greater rather than less attention in the next decade. This problem is all the more delicate because of the comparative youth of the majority of the academic bodies and the high rate of change in personnel. In the immediate future these conditions are likely to continue because the colleges are reaching the point where a great proportion of the more senior and founder members of the academic staff reach retiring age or are moving on to other spheres of activity. In general, senates (or their equivalents) have greater responsibility implicitly if not explicitly than do corresponding bodies in Britain. It is therefore all the more important that they be fully informed on all college matters, and that they be prepared to provide clear-cut advice when required.

This responsibility for participation in college government has sometimes led young recruits to the academic staff to become involved in committee work to an extent which has threatened their scholastic duties. Distinction in committee work is, however, an indifferent qualification in scholarship, and how to keep a reasonable balance between apprenticeship in college government, some might say politics, and scholarship is not easy to determine.

The problem has recently been commented upon in the general context of college government and administration by Dr Mellanby, the first Principal of University College, Ibadan : ' I am afraid I have never felt that academic administration is of more than secondary importance. . . . Administration is inevitable. It should try to be efficient ; it should make sure it is unobtrusive. Its job should be to see that the academic work of the college goes on as smoothly as possible, remembering that the college cannot live without the academic members however much their habits may irritate the administrators, whereas the academic staff at least imagine they will get on quite well with no administrators. The position is more complicated than I have ever indicated, for not only do some university administrators suffer from delusions of grandeur, but members of the academic staff often fancy themselves as administrators. Instead of getting on with their teaching and research, there are many professors and lecturers who delight in interfering with the day-to-day running of the college, its office and other academic departments than their own. . . . I think the reason for this behaviour is that administration requires so much less concentration than research, and is much easier than devoting one's time to the needs of students, so it appeals to those who fear they are not making a success of academic work, or who are downright idle.'[1]

The way in which the university has been added to the educational structure in the respective territories is a credit to all concerned in the work, and the initial success of the enterprise is remarkable. The problems lying immediately ahead are likely to prove more taxing than have been those of foundation-laying. The satisfactory solving of the new problems will call for greater rather than diminished co-operation between the old and the new universities, between the people of the new nations and the imperial nations of yesterday. What began as sponsorship from the Mother Country is now becoming another aspect of partnership. At the same time the need for further new universities is demanding yet more by way of sponsorship.[2]

These new possibilities raise a variety of issues. Financially, they may limit the resources available to existing institutions in the future. The abortive proposals made to share professional schools might with advantage be re-examined. The concept of separate universities as opposed to federations of colleges in some regions would also appear to be due for re-examination.

[1] K. Mellanby, *The Birth of Nigeria's University*, Methuen, 1958
[2] Since this essay was originally published Fourah Bay College, Sierra Leone, has been granted a University College Charter, in Eastern Nigeria the University of Nigeria has been founded under the joint sponsorship of Michigan State University and the University of London, the Ashby Committee has recommended the establishment of a university for Northern Nigeria and another to be located in Lagos. The College of Arts, Science and Technology, Nairobi has been renamed the Royal College and is being developed as a constituent college of the University of East Africa, which will be a federal university consisting of Makerere College, Uganda, the Royal College, Nairobi and the University College of Tanganyika. In Malaya a second university college unit has been built up at Kuala Lumpur, and in Basutoland, a private foundation, University College of Pius XII has been established in affiliation with the University of South Africa.

If the latter approach is to be ruled out, then the need for consultative machinery between the new universities, as well as general membership of the Commonwealth Universities Bureau, will need review. The value of the first faculty conference (Education) held at Salisbury, Rhodesia, in September 1958, which was attended by representatives of all the new British university institutions in Africa south of the Sahara and north of the Limpopo, with the addition of representatives from the Belgian Congo, Basutoland and Natal, pointed clearly to a new need, which at present in Africa is being met in part through the generosity of the Leverhulme Trust.

The staffing needs of existing and future foundations will continue to make considerable demands upon the world field of university workers. This calls for a study of both needs and resources. In this, and in the general study of future higher educational needs, counterparts of the Inter-University Council for Higher Education Overseas could be brought into being in other countries participating in similar activities, thus providing for more satisfactory international collaboration. It is essential that this be recognised as primarily a task for the university world, and not as just another exercise in international cultural relations.

The establishment of university institutions was not the only outcome of the review of higher educational needs that took place between 1943 and 1945. The Asquith Commission limited its consideration of professional technical education to engineering. But the West African Commission majority report recommended the appointment of three officers, (a) to survey existing facilities for technical and commercial training in consultation with those planning economic development, (b) to establish technical institutes and (c) to supervise the future development of technical education. The members of the Commission who signed the minority report did not dissent from these recommendations. The Secretary of State for the Colonies set up a committee to advise him on the development of Colonial Colleges of Arts, Science and Technology. That committee (now the Council for Overseas Colleges of Arts, Science and Technology) is providing

33

the same guidance in the field of technical education that the Inter-University Council provides in the field of university education. With the additional assistance of local committees the Council for Overseas Colleges of Arts, Science and Technology has brought into being the Kumasi College of Arts, Science and Technology in the Gold Coast; the Nigerian College of Arts, Science and Technology; the Royal Technical College of East Africa; and it has assisted in the reconstruction of Fourah Bay College, Sierra Leone, provided guidance in the development of facilities in Malaya and made its advice available elsewhere.

These institutions have had their own peculiar difficulties, arising in part from the fact that they represented something different from the traditional technical institute in Britain, and in part from ambiguity about the kind of objectives to be pursued. The assessment of the position made by Sir David Lindsay Keir in 1956 is still valid. In a presidential address to the Association of Technical Institutes, he then said :

I do not want to enter upon the general and greatly vexed question whether, or how, such studies should everywhere form a part of technological education. It is quite sufficient as regards such education overseas, to resort to special pleading. We in this country are, when all is said and done, in a strong position for dealing with the educational problems of our technological age. We have sustained its impact gradually, our social structure though sometimes dislocated has never been destroyed : we are sustained by a powerful tradition in education in skilled craftsmanship and in professional and business life : and our values in personal conduct and social obligation, though eroded here and there, are still secure against the main stresses. In the oversea territories, few, if any, of these reassurances can be found. The impact, abrupt and severe, has often fallen on societies unprotected by our defences. No social organisation has held out quite intact. Some, with all the beliefs and sanctions they imply and uphold, have collapsed. If there is to be a rebuilding, it must be through men to whom a profession, trade or industry involves not just a mastery of technical processes, but of a whole way of life. To provide this rounded and complete education seems to me the purpose of a college of arts, science and technology as we have conceived it. It is independent, residential,

34

selective, concerned with higher education only, and aimed at the same standards as ours, chiefly because it is intended to uphold the same professional ideas of competence, liberality of mind and integrity of character as we cherish at home. To bring that about, such colleges must do more than we attempt or find necessary here, at any rate as things now are.

The objections must be frankly faced. The colleges may be held not to satisfy the most serious need of the oversea territories, the need for recruitment into the lower and intermediate grades, where the skills of the artisan, the clerk, the technician, the supervisor and inspector, so greatly wanted, are so desperately scarce. They may be reckoned unduly costly in proportion to their immediate output of qualified men. They may be criticised for encroaching on the sphere which belongs to universities. To these objections I believe there are valid replies. The need for technical training at lower levels is so widespeard that it must be dealt with on a decentralised local basis, as is being done in the technical institutes and trade schools, and not concentrated inconveniently and expensively in one place. The case for attempting every grade of technical education in the same institutions is seductive but erroneous. Of course, the cost per student of an institution for higher education alone must be heavy at first ; but it will fall as the number of those qualified for entry increases. And as to the line of demarcation between the university colleges and the colleges of technology, there is no need to reproduce in the oversea territories that dualism in higher education which through the accidents of history we have evolved here at home.

Already the line is getting a bit blurred. The colleges of arts, science and technology were at first thought of as working on a lower level, as feeders to the university colleges. This conception soon gave place to one of parity : both kinds of college are to provide higher education, and nothing else, each in its own field. But the two fields can only be roughly delimited, more to meet practical needs than to comply with abstract principles.

One direction in which co-operation rather than delimitation is being explored is in engineering training. In June 1957 the Council of the University College, Ibadan, revealed that agreement had been reached with the Council of the Nigerian College of Arts, Science and Technology to establish a Faculty of Engineering at the Zaria Branch of the latter college. This collaboration might be pursued in respect of teacher training, the fine arts and administration.

In the West Indies the report of a mission on the needs of the Caribbean area in respect of higher technological education recommended :

> That the University College of the West Indies should proceed to a Faculty of Engineering ; that a block of laboratories should be built in the University precincts to be used jointly by the University College of the West Indies for its degree courses and by the Kingston Technical College for its advanced courses in engineering ; and that the governing bodies of the two colleges should at once set up a committee to work out the details of this proposal.[1]

The idea of a joint-users scheme received the approval of the Quinquennial Advisory Committee of the University College, although they were unable to visualise the College taking any practical steps to establish a Faculty of Engineering during the forthcoming quinquennium. It is clear that with imagination and mutual understanding the development of the two types of institutions might help to avoid the dualism which through the accidents of history has come about in Britain.

The general comments made about finance, staffing, research and staff-student relationships in the university institutions are in varying degree applicable to the technological institutions. In public relations the technological institutions are to some extent handicapped by the comparative lack of local industrial and technological advisers. As remarked by Sir Stephen Luke in the 1957 Report on Development and Welfare, ' Much has been said about the lack of expertise in the technical field ; no-one had attempted to state in precise terms the nature or the extent of the shortage.'[2] But this is a handicap that in the long run might prove an advantage, in that as local industrial and techno-logical development takes place there should grow up an intimate

[1] *University College of the West Indies, Principal's Report, 1956-57*, Kingston 1957

[2] Sir Stephen Luke, *Report on Development and Welfare in the West Indies*, 1957

relation between the new industrial leaders and the teaching institutions that should help considerably in the formulation of research policy, and in the balance of emphasis in the teaching programmes.

One field of work to which special attention has been drawn recently, and which undoubtedly offers special scope for co-operation between the technological institutions and the University College Departments of Education, is in the training of technical teachers. At the second Inter-African Conference on Industrial, Commercial and Agricultural Education held at Luanda in 1957 under the auspices of the Commission for Technical Co-operation in Africa South of the Sahara, the opinion was recorded that ' the success of any scheme of vocational education and training is necessarily dependent upon the quality of the teaching staff ', and the following recommendations were made : ' that all teachers in vocational education should have contact with the industrial world, and that those specifically concerned with the teaching of any craft should have had industrial experience in the craft taught ; that arrangements should be made for the periodical release of teaching staff in order that they may renew their acquaintance with modern industrial processes and manufacturing methods. The arrangements should provide for the continuation of the teacher's salary and for adequate maintenance allowances ; the Conference finally recommended that all vocational teachers should be required to undertake some form of pedagogical training which should make provision for supplementary practical training where industrial experience is lacking. In addition, short courses should be held from time to time for the discussion and consideration of new teaching techniques.' [1]

It is to be noted that the provision of facilities to meet the last of these recommendations is already under discussion between the Royal Technical College of East Africa and the Makerere College Department of Education. An experimental short in-service course for technical teachers has recently been

[1] *Education : Inter-African Conference, Luanda, 1957*, C.C.T.A./C.S.A., Bukavu 1958

arranged by the University College of Ghana Institute of Education at the invitation of the Ministry of Education technical branch.

In 1925 the Advisory Committee on Native Education in the British Tropical African Dependencies in their first memorandum visualised that ' (Education) systems should be established which, although varying with local conditions, would provide elementary education for boys and girls, secondary education of several types, technical and vocational education, institutions of higher education which might eventually develop into universities.' [1] The problems of finance, staff, courses, research, administration and public relations which have been referred to indicate the extent to which higher education has been developed as part of the systems visualised in 1925. A review of the proposals of the Higher Education Commissions in the light of what has happened since might provide material for criticism, but such criticism (as has indeed been indulged in to some extent in certain quarters) implies that the Commissions, the Inter-University Council and the Council for Overseas Colleges of Arts, Science and Technology should have been crystal-ball readers. In fact, each institution that has come into being during this period has been developed with vigour and imagination. Unforeseen factors have created difficulties which, in some cases, will call for the utmost wisdom and perseverance and will offer fresh scope for co-operation and partnership. Men and women from these institutions are already taking responsible positions in their own societies. In some territories they are watched critically and their limitations and weaknesses are sometimes unkindly exposed. In other territories they are being accepted as a new *élite*. In all territories they represent the beginnings of a new stream of intellectual and administrative manpower to the advantage of the new nations and the comity of nations as a whole.

---

[1] *Educational Policy in British Tropical Africa*, Cmd. 2374, H.M.S.O., 1925

3

Anglo-American University Co-operation in the Changing World

Exchange and co-operation have always been features of university life which for the most part have occurred through the movement of individuals rather than through deliberate policy decisions. Any deliberate planning at the organisational level calls for analysis of purposes and objectives and for an examination of procedures and techniques.

In this section there is provided (i) a brief analysis of the function of a university in relation to the present and future life of society, apart from the conservation and pursuit of knowledge and its academic dissemination; (ii) an examination of the role that American and British universities have to play not only in respect of each other's society, but also in respect of those societies that are variously designated by such terms as under-developed, emergent, new nations and the like; (iii) a brief account of the contemporary British university system and the part it is at present playing in international co-operation, together with a brief comment on American participation as seen through the eyes of a person whose tradition and experience is British; and (iv) an attempt to examine some of the problems and difficulties of co-operation, whether planned or unplanned; and a personal approach to the solution of some of these problems.

II

The world we live in is one world. In spite of the persistence of the anachronistic apparatus of nationalism, old and new, technological change has made it impossible for men to live any longer in isolated groups. Assuming that it is a function of institutions of higher education to serve as 'central power stations for generating and distributing the voltage and the current for the forces of " progress " ',[1] then it is clear that the British and American universities must co-operate with each other and with the institutions created to serve less fortunate members of the world community. However differently the specific nature and purposes of the university are understood (and many of these are significant), there are areas of agreement which are strengthened by co-operation ; they make it possible for individual institutions to participate in international affairs and to assist developments in other countries.

There are considerable differences of detail in the beliefs held about the nature and purpose of a university in different parts of the world. But, whatever the differences, there are certain characteristics that are accepted to a greater or lesser degree everywhere :

1 The university is a social institution existing to gather and to disseminate knowledge.

2 It has responsibility for synthesising and interpreting the facts that are accumulated. This task has become much more difficult in recent times because of the growth of many new fields of knowledge and because of the rate of the accumulation of new data in the old disciplines.

3 The university has a responsibility to the community for the moral as well as the intellectual well-being of the students and this responsibility transcends local responsibilities.

4 The university has a responsibility for training specialists and professional workers, a responsibility which stretches beyond provincial and national boundaries. In present-day conditions this implies responsibility for those human beings not yet equipped to provide special and vocational education at the university level.

5 The university must be free both to explore and to profess,

---

[1] Charles Grant Robertson, *The British Universities*, Methuen, London 1944

and this freedom must be encouraged by society and be clearly demonstrated to exist. This characteristic of the university is the better established, maintained and demonstrated when close relationships exist between individual universities. In initiation and growth this responsibility is one that needs support and stimulus best derived from the success of other institutions.

It is in the above terms that it is valid to claim that the British and the American universities should be concerned to promote co-operation between themselves and with the new institutions serving other communities.

Overriding the validity of the theoretical arguments in favour of co-operation, there is the practical and immediate fact of the need for help that has been sought and is being given to foundations established in Asia, Africa and the Caribbean during the last decade and a half.

III

The British universities have already been involved in oversea co-operation in a systematic fashion on a large scale since 1945. Even earlier than that, two of them undertook oversea commitments. In 1876 Fourah Bay College, Sierra Leone, was affiliated to the University of Durham, and given university college status, thus being in a position to prepare students for the Durham degree in arts and the Diploma in Theology. Similar status had been granted by Durham to an institution in the West Indies in 1875. The Charter of Incorporation of the University of London granted in 1836 required the University to examine external students as well as internal students. This provision was taken advantage of by individuals and institutions, and has been the instrument which has enabled such institutions to make university teaching their major preoccupation and thus to claim university college status and eventually independent university status. Commenting upon this arrangement in an oration delivered in

1959 at the London School of Economics and Political Science, Sir Alexander Carr-Saunders remarked :

The story is of a kind familiar in our history ; there was no plan for the foundings of new universities ; as problems arose, means of overcoming them were devised. But the story has received an interpretation of a kind so familiar in our history, that is of discovering special merit in the procedures upon which we have stumbled. The special merit imputed to this procedure is that, before a college becomes a university, it is always good for it to undergo a period of tutelage during which students are prepared for a degree of another university, or, as in the latest case, the college is sponsored by other universities.[1]

In 1945 a similar method of establishing new universities in the British dependent territories overseas was deliberately planned after searching consideration of the problem. The work of the Royal Commission on Higher Education in the Colonies and of its ancillary committees resulted in the establishment of the Inter-University Council for Higher Education in the Colonies, consisting of representatives of the English universities. Its function is to give guidance to the new university institutions it was proposed to establish in Asia, Africa and the Caribbean. The assistance rendered by the Inter-University Council is to give advice, both to the new colleges and the United Kingdom Government, in so far as it is sought in matters of policy and in the selection and appointment of staff. In order to provide for the tutelage of these new institutions, the resources of the University of London were harnessed to the needs of the colleges through a planned system of special relationships.

By such a relationship, subject to certain safeguards, students who satisfied the requirements might be awarded degrees of that university. It was intended that the special relationship should include the joint approval of syllabuses and examination requirements with proper attention to local conditions. The commission stipulated that degree-granting powers could be conferred on a new institution only when the staff had obtained adequate experience of work of a

[1] Sir Alexander Carr-Saunders, *English Universities Today*, London School of Economics and Political Science, London 1960

university standard, that their conditions of work allowed for the active prosecution of research or other original work, and that a substantial number of students had completed satisfactorily the courses leading to degrees in a sufficient range of subjects.[1]

The period of tutelage originally envisaged has been substantially reduced, in part because of changes in the political status of particular territories (university tutelage appears to be incompatible with political independence) and in part because of the success of the procedures adopted. Some persons have been and still are critical of the extent to which the new colleges seem to have followed too closely the London pattern. Some have seen in the arrangements the hand of continuing imperial control. Failure to evolve startlingly different syllabuses and methods, if there has been such failure, is due much more to insufficiency of knowledge about local phenomena and to the simple fact that, at undergraduate level, most university courses are similar anyway. There may be better ways of giving aid and co-operation, there certainly are different ways, and there is scope for experiment, but the persons who designed the Inter-University Council and the scheme of special relationship can be reasonably satisfied with the solution they produced.

One of the important factors that has contributed to the success of the scheme of Special Relationship has been the amount of informal exchange of views and experiences that has been possible between the teachers and administrators of the new foundations and those in London. This process of informal consultation is of great value in preparing for the initiation of formal action, and frequently continues to the interim solution of matters that are temporarily of great importance but hardly deserve the attention of the full machinery of consultation and decision.

That there are several ways of going about the creation of new universities has been demonstrated in England most recently by the manner in which the University of North Staffordshire was established in 1949 in response to local demand, under the

[1] L. J. Lewis, ' Higher Education in the Oversea Territories 1948–58 ', *British Journal of Educational Studies*, Vol. VIII, No. 1, Faber, London, November 1959

sponsorship of the Universities of Manchester, Birmingham and Oxford. This represents two departures from the accepted method of establishing new universities in England. In the first place the authority to grant degrees was given to the new institution from its inception and did not involve a long period in which the students were external candidates for degrees of the University of London. In the second place the giving of guidance is accepted as a responsibility to be shared by several established universities. Another pointer to different ways of doing things is to be seen in the proposals for developing the Royal Technical College of East Africa into a university college as part of a Federal University of East Africa, in which academic and professional courses shall have equal status. The proposals for providing professional and technical studies together with the traditional academic studies represents a departure from the dual system in England where university and technological studies are by tradition provided in separate institutions.

Co-operation has succeeded in giving confidence to the persons directly involved in the making of the new colleges as well as to the local community. It has also made it possible for teaching staffs, drawn from a great diversity of universities, to arrive at a common canon to work by. Through the continuity of working contact with teachers from London and through regular service on examination boards and participation in staff selection meetings, there has been insurance against the comparative isolation and parochialism that might easily have dominated the lives of the new colleges and militated against their developing a sense of equality and membership with the university world at large.

In England, whilst there are various methods of developing and furthering university institutions, there is a common authority exercised by the University Grants Committee. This body, consisting of senior university teachers and of former teachers, is an independent body which considers the requests for financial aid from the universities to the government. By visitations and by examination of documentary evidence submitted it assesses the claims of the individual universities, and collates them for submission *in toto* to the Treasury. Because of the nature of its relationship with the universities on the one hand and the Treasury on the other, it safeguards the autonomy of the universities, whilst at the same time providing assurance that public funds made available for higher education are efficiently and wisely administered. By the way it works, government officials are saved from any embarrassment that could easily arise if they were required to examine in detail the university claims for assistance, whilst at the same time the universities without embarrassment are made continually aware of their obligations in using public funds.

Whilst the Inter-University Council is purely advisory and is a separate body from the University Grants Committee, it is able to make available the experience and knowledge embodied in the University Grants Committee because of the overlap of personnel.

The autonomy of the university, as has already been indicated, is fundamental to that academic freedom which is believed to be vital to learning. In all the countries where political independence is a new experience, political leaders are particularly sensitive to criticism. The sensitivity may reflect anxiety concerning their own ability to maintain the control in their own hands. It is also a sign of political immaturity. In the British and former British dependent territories the newly established university colleges are largely dependent upon the government for their finance. In spite of the granting of legal autonomy, there have been occasions when government has been tempted to interfere with and restrict the freedom of the university and of individual members of the university. The Inter-University Council has through its own independent status been able to give support to the new colleges in this matter. An illustration of this point occurs in the 1957 report of the Commission on the University of Malta :

> A university, if it be properly so called, has objectives more distant and more difficult to achieve than even the important purpose of professional education. It must seek to advance learning in the fields with which it is concerned and in general pursue fundamental

knowledge and fundamental criticism in a fashion which sets it apart from and may even at times set it, or some of its members, in opposition to the prevailing disposition of the community to which it belongs. That service calls for expenditure only partly related to currently visible needs, and for a climate of opinion which is ready to tolerate and even to respect a minority.[1]

Another facet of the issue, namely the control of finance, has been approached in a manner which reflects the function in Britain of the University Grants Committee. It is not possible to set up a replica of the U.G.C. in the countries where the new university colleges have been established, but the concept of independent machinery for reconciling the conflicting claims of national needs and university autonomy that it has demonstrated has been accepted in principle, even though the full implications of the procedure have not been generally understood. However, the greatest weakness in this respect probably lies less in the lack of understanding on the part of key administrators and politicians than in the lack of an informed public. Referring to the University in its English context, Dr C. W. Logan, in his annual report on the University of London in 1957, said :

In the outside world there is, I fear, a great lack of understanding of what the University is, what it stands for and what it does. The responsibility for this sad state of affairs rests largely on the University itself which could justly be accused of going out of its way to hide its light under a bushel. It is vitally necessary that the problems with which the University is faced—and they are many and complex—should be more fully comprehended and the points at issue more clearly grasped than is at present the case.[2]

The situation in the underdeveloped countries with which we are concerned is such that there are few people who have any comprehension of what a university is. This is exacerbated by

[1] The Royal University of Malta, *Report of the Commission, July 1957*, para. 6, Inter-University Council for Higher Education Overseas, London
[2] C. W. Logan, *University of London, Report of the Principal, 1956–57*, London 1957

the fact that the overwhelming majority of the academic members of the university colleges are expatriates who possess little or no knowledge of the ways of life and thought of the local people, and who show little appreciation of the need to develop good public relations and to interpret the purpose of the university to the society in which they find themselves. The necessity for so doing is not easily grasped by scholars brought up in a tradition that sees the university as a self-contained system, not anxious to make an impact on the outside world and still hardly affected by it. This tradition, which persists more strongly than is sometimes realised, is a source of irritation to the local politicians and to the young Asian, African and Caribbean university teachers. Because they are the first of their own people to become university teachers they are in great demand for all kinds of activities outside the college. In these circumstances their main work, namely research and teaching, may suffer seriously. Difficulties have also arisen out of British concern for academic standards that has frequently appeared to be not very relevant to the practical needs of the societies the new universities are established to serve.

IV

The question of academic standards is one which has assumed much greater importance in the last few years since the advent of American participation in education in Africa. It was first discussed in a quasi-official way in Washington in 1949, when advantage was taken of a visit made by a group of British educationists from Africa to share experience with American educationists and to see something of the American work in Negro education. At that time little was achieved. The most recent contribution to the subject is that provided by Bernard Mellor of the British Embassy, Washington, D.C., in an article ' American Degrees and British Students '[1]. Commenting upon the article, the editor of *Oversea Education* (pp. 145-46), W. E. F. Ward, writes :

[1] *Oversea Education*, Vol. XXX, No. 4, January 1959, pp. 147-59 (London, H.M.S.O.).

For some years past, the question—American Degrees and British Students—has had a very practical importance in British oversea territories, for an increasing number of their students go to America for their University education, and in due course they demand that their American degrees be suitably recognised. The authorities are in a quandary. It would be simple if it were an M.A. from Harvard or Yale ; but often it is a first degree from a college which the authorities do not know, and they have no means of judging how much the degree is worth. This is a dangerous situation. It is natural for the returned graduate to assume that his B.A. is just as good as anybody else's ; he has his natural pride in his American Alma Mater, and he cannot be expected to know that not all university degrees are of the same academic standing. If, as a result of such enquiries as they are able to make, the authorities regretfully tell him they cannot recognise him as entitled to graduate status, it is not surprising if he sometimes jumps to unpleasant conclusions about their motives.

Important as the matter is for the individual, it is in some ways of greater importance at the present time for the institutions themselves. This is not so much because of the problems of accreditation that are involved, but because discussions about equivalence obscure the fact that there is a difference between British and American aims. British aims, traditionally, are essentially the preservation, advancement and propagation of learning. The American aims are directed more specifically to education for citizenship. Herein lies one of the problems of American participation in the already established educational systems derived from the British tradition. A person who has taken a first degree in an American university in a relatively wide range of subjects, many of which are specifically concerned with fitting the individual for the American way of life, is frequently handicapped when seeking professional recognition for purposes of employment in British institutions or those based upon the British pattern. What is required, where people educated in one culture are to be employed in teaching in another culture served by an education system derived from yet another tradition, is exact definition of the teaching requirements, in terms of the content and purpose of the courses and the ways in which the teaching is done. At the same time it must be understood that the general attitudes that result from the discipline of university studies are more important than the details of the subject matter. A summary of the differences, provided by G. F. Kneller, may serve to put the matter in proper perspective and to indicate in what way interpretation is possible :

> In the first place, British university entrants are usually one year older and have attended secondary school a year or two longer than their American confrères. They are more highly selected, both as they proceed through the secondary school and in consequence of a highly developed entrance, or matriculation, examination system. Higher education is not simply an extension of secondary school training ; it involves not so much a continuance of general education as a concentrated program of ' reading ' a certain specialty. In a sense, the first-year and possibly the second-year graduate at a British university may more nearly be compared with a third-year student in an American college, with certain added qualities characteristic of the American graduate school, particularly as regards individual responsibility for scholarly production. In assessing British and American higher education the following data should be taken into account: (1) The fairer comparison omits the accomplishment of the first two years or so of the American college. (2) The British make a distinction between higher education and what has recently been termed ' further ' education ; that is, the type of training that takes place in organised institutions of learning beyond school-leaving age (fifteen or sixteen). (3) The type, quality and intensity of work accomplished are matters largely of national educational preference.[1]

Much the most important of the factors enumerated is that of national preference. British and Americans must both recognise that in any effort to solve the problems of co-operation, individual or institutional, this is probably the factor most difficult to deal with. National preferences give rise to prejudices that are not easily recognised or admitted, and they can result

[1] George F. Kneller, *Higher Learning in Britain*, p. 225, University of California Press, Berkeley, California, 1955

49

in clashes of opinion that prevent people from working together. But it is not only the differences of British and American origin that have to be recognised. When working together in a third country both British and Americans must remember that there are local national preferences to be considered. The value placed upon qualifications has been important in the past. With the increase of the numbers of Americans and of American-trained persons in educational systems essentially British in character, interpretation of qualifications will become increasingly important. Whereas doubts about American qualifications has, in the past, appeared to be an expression of British prejudice exercised by reactionary imperialists, the questioning, in the future, will come from local personnel, who are already beginning to demonstrate that they have a vested interest in British standards which they regard as a part of their inheritance. The persons who have with much enthusiasm organised the large-scale movement of East Africans to the United States for further studies have not understood this. As a result their well-intentioned generosity may have unfortunate consequences. For the most part the East Africans chosen to be taken to the U.S.A. failed to gain admission to Makerere because they are not qualified to do so. If they succeed in obtaining a university qualification in the United States they will expect to get the same kind of appointment as their contemporaries from Makerere College. If they do obtain appointments on an equal footing with the Makerere graduate, being initially less able persons, their inadequacies will be blamed upon their qualifications and as a result disparaging comparisons will be made. Even where political leadership is wholeheartedly in favour of American participation, as in the case of Eastern Nigeria, in practice individuals may find that political enthusiasm for their presence may not be matched by professional zeal for their co-operation.

As has already been said, the most effective way of dealing with the difficulties inherent in this problem is to define more precisely the kind of assistance required, and to describe the conditions in which the individual will be working. The disappointment that some Americans, who have undertaken educational work in West Africa through the good offices of the African-American Institute have suffered could have been avoided if there had been better knowledge and understanding of the academic, administrative and social circumstances involved. The lesson to be learned from British-administrative and from American-missionary experience lies in the amount of preparation over and above professional training that is necessary for the worker going overseas. This preparation must include training for adjustment to indigenous circumstances and familiarisation with the modes of thought and the methods of working of government officials.

Recognition that there is, more often than not, a real difference in content between initial educational qualifications of British and American trained persons does not necessarily mean that measurable equivalence cannot be established. Instead of sterile argument about 'standards' a constructive attitude could be inculcated by giving consideration to what is wanted in particular circumstances, what is available and what is needed to supplement it. In addition, there must be readiness to make modifications in the requirements as far as is possible. Much of the mutual irritation that has been engendered up to the present would rapidly disappear if all parties deliberately sought to be constructive in these matters.

When attempting to equate particular qualifications, it must be remembered that the approach to higher education in Britain and in America is different and consequently the individuals trained there will have different outlooks. But in addition British and American trained persons alike must be able to recognise that both traditions are intrusive in the under-developed country we seek to serve. Whilst it is true that in British and former British territories the British tradition is at present paramount, the rates and complexities of the changes taking place are creating different needs and will result in modifications of the British tradition as locally interpreted. This will have to be taken into account by British and American alike, and attention will have to be paid to problems of orientation to an extent that has not been practised in the past by either British or American institutions seeking to serve the under-developed territories by training recruits to the service.

When American universities introduce courses in comparative education and international studies they will need to realise that persons trained for service overseas should study not only some other academic disciplines but also understand the institutions and social patterns derivative from the former imperialist power in addition to those derivative from the indigenous culture.

V

The training referred to in the preceding paragraphs is of a kind that the home university is concerned with in a preparatory sense, but for which it does not have continuing responsibility once the training is completed and the persons trained have begun their professional duties. But there is a category of worker for whom the home university has a continuing responsibility, namely persons seconded temporarily to do a particular job and then to return to the home university. Such persons are judged not only as themselves but also as representing their own university.

In British experience in Africa the visiting professor from the United States has been, without exception, an asset to the local university colleges. On the other hand the itinerant research worker has not always been an unqualified success. A number of considerations bear upon this aspect of co-operation. The order in which they are commented upon in the following paragraphs is not an order of importance because the factors vary in significance with the individual person and situation.

One group of difficulties and irritations is directly the consequence of the zeal, exuberance and lack of experience of the young research worker on his first oversea assignment. A project which, when discussed in the study of the Dean or Professor in the U.S.A. or elaborated in a paper submitted to a foundation, seemed to be of great significance may well appear, in the eyes of teachers and administrators in an African institution, to be fomewhat remote from the more immediate needs. The zealous pursuit of officials, businessmen, traders, missionaries and the like for information is a fresh and necessary activity for the young research worker : but for some of the recipients of the inquiries it is a time-consuming irritation that happens too frequently. When such inquiries are carried out by means of questionnaires, tape-recorders, cameras and other 'informal machinery', suspicion hardens. The addition of gratuitous criticism of colonialism and imperialism, and undiluted adulation of the local politicians or the traditional 'culture', arouses chauvinism in representatives of the former colonial power and irritates scholar and administrator alike. If the bright young thing attempts to intrude in the government of the institution to which he is temporarily attached, and offers criticism of how its affairs are managed, public and social relations are unlikely to be improved.

This is, of course, a caricature. Unfortunately it is made up of an incident here, an incident there, each small in itself but by 'bush telegraph' exaggerated in importance until its shadow overcasts regions far beyond the tiny origin. Young British research workers commit similar gaffes, but get dealt with more quickly and rigorously by their British colleagues.

What is called for in this aspect of temporary university work overseas is early and continuing consultation and careful planning of the arrangements. The young man who goes on a research assignment to Ghana will find different living and working conditions from those he would find at Salisbury or Makerere, and certainly considerable differences from his home circumstances. What is an unwelcome topic for research at one place is recognised as a priority at another. One faculty in a college will have excellent working relations with local people, and officials in trade and industry. In the same college another faculty will be 'ivory-towered' to a degree that is medieval. The enthusiasm of an individual member of a department for some aspect of his discipline or for the relevant social situation may not be shared by any other persons. These matters are important in any situation, but their importance takes on quite a different significance in institutions that are new, not yet welded into organic units, not yet part of the community they are intended to serve.

This problem can be tackled a number of ways. The difficulties and irritations can be ignored and, in so far as they involve former imperialist personnel, can be regarded as temporary, belonging to an age that is quickly passing. They can be accepted as an inevitable consequence of a ' crash ' programme. But a more* positive approach is possible and ought to be attempted.

In the first place, the individuals at both ends should be more carefully advised about personal and public relations. Secondly, more time should be given in advance to systematic assessment of the proposals and of the procedures to be followed. Wherever possible, arrangements should be made to report the outcomes of the work to the local institutions and organisations. This is particularly important because, more often than not, the impression is given that resources available to the visiting worker are far in excess of those that would be available to a local worker in the same circumstances, and that the purpose is merely for the visitor to acquire the kudos attendant on a Ph.D. or a publication.

The machinery of consultation within any one region, e.g. West Africa, should be established at three levels : (1) exchange of information between institutions about research programmes and projects, and about the resources available ; (2) more detailed exchange of information at the faculty level ; and (3) more consultation leading to orientation of the individual worker to the specific situation. Some consultation can be effectively arranged using existing facilities and, at the level of individual contact, some excellent relations have been established, but a great deal more needs to be done. The establishment of satisfactory exchange of information at these three levels would make it much easier to develop Anglo-American and local co-operation in applying joint resources to teaching and research.

In some disciplines, e.g. the social and political sciences, the relations between government departments and the university departments can be delicate. The differences between British

54

and American approaches need careful examination and interpretation, for not only are relations between institutions involved,
but there are often political overtones which can be extremely
delicate and not readily understood by lay persons. In empha-
sising the need for special attention to this aspect of relations
between the foreign universities and new local foundations, it
has to be remembered that major disagreements are almost
invariably triggered off by, if not created by, incidents of minor
importance and often involve individuals whose own standing is
not very important.

A different kind of problem is created when a purely American
form of training is brought into an education system based on
the British pattern. The Ohio University experiment attempted
along these lines at Ibadan in Western Nigeria is an example of
the misfortune which can attend the most enthusiastic and best-
intentioned efforts when the need for interpretative understanding is overlooked. Institutions established earlier by American
missionaries have experience of the problems of relating American
practice to British conditions that does not appear to be valued
by individuals and organisations sponsored by new sources of
philanthropy emanating from the United States. This is all the
more astonishing when it is remembered that the Phelps-Stokes
Commissions on education in Africa in 1921 to 1923 enunciated
explicitly principles of adaptation and co-operation which have
influenced African education ever since. The reports still offer
sound guidance about planning educational development.[1]

When in 1945 extension of university facilities in the colonial
territories was proposed, the responsibility for the policy lay
with the imperial power. Local indigenous support was derived
from a very limited element of the population. What local
knowledge of the nature of university education existed was
almost entirely British in derivation. In the fifteen years that
have passed circumstances have greatly changed. The concern
for university education has increased among the local people.

[1] Thomas Jesse Jones, *Education in Africa*, Phelps-Stokes Fund, New York
1922; and Thomas Jesse Jones, *Education in East Africa*, Phelps-Stokes Fund,
New York 1924

55

There is much greater understanding that there are other ways of providing university education than according to the established British pattern. It is also recognised, in some quarters, that further developments are likely to require assistance beyond the resources that Britain and the local government can immediately make available. And there is to some extent an interest in American ways, drawn in part from experience, in part from secondary sources that have something of the fashion-value of newness. In addition they have promise of being specially relevant to the needs of the new nations. The two-way traffic of scholars is stimulating this interest and it is likely to lead to American universities being involved in government projects such as the setting up of the Eastern Region Nigeria University. These developments will give rise to a number of problems, essentially ' political ' in character.

It is, of course, assumed that in these circumstances the United States government and the United States universities will accept responsibility for giving aid. In whatever manner it is done, there must be assurance that no strings are attached to the aid given. This is a surety that has been unequivocal in the British assistance given through grants from the Colonial Development and Welfare Fund. Because of the method of giving aid no anxieties have been felt about freedom for either the local governments or the local university colleges. This freedom was demonstrated in Ghana, when though there were differences between the university authorities and the national government, these did not prevent the national government from inviting the Inter-University Council to provide specialist assistance in reviewing the finance of the university college.

The complex of the many publicly and privately supported institutions that makes up the United States university world clearly does not permit of an imitation of the Inter-University Council. But it should be possible to establish a body representative of the American universities that could accept administrative and academic responsibility for channelling Federal, State and private aid to other territories in a fashion that would lend authority without trespassing upon the rights of either the

American institutions or of the institutions and governments of the recipient nations. The acceptance of the authority of such a body as the vehicle of aid will be dependent upon its representative character in respect of academic responsibilities and its independence in respect of the home government. In so far as the ' contract' procedure followed by the Federal government in using university facilities implies a dependence by the latter upon the government, there are almost certain to be occasions when suspicions are aroused in the receiving country. In this respect, despite occasional remarks about Ford Foundation ' spies ', because of the manner in which this and other American foundations have given aid to the new university colleges, it has been accepted without seeking for ulterior motives. A possible line of development would be the establishment of a Universities Advisory Council, whose duties would be to advise on such matters concerning university development as may be referred to the Council by the Federal government, by oversea governments and by individual American institutions. Executive machinery for putting into effect any advice given should be provided by university institutions on invitation, accepting responsibility individually or in co-operation. Public funds allocated for such purposes would be granted directly to the operating institution or institutions for programmes approved by the Council. In the event of difficulties arising in political or academic terms, the Council could be used by recipient institutions and governments with full assurance that the advice would be independent and authoritative. In the event of responsibility being accepted for total sponsoring of a new institution, nomination of a representative of the Council to the governing body of the new institution could provide the means of personal contact between the Council, the academic and administrative membership of the university college and the lay members of the governing body. This would be at once educative and reassuring. The greatest danger to co-operative enterprise is provincialism which, out of ignorance, breeds suspicion. The purpose of aid that is provided without adequate machinery for regular and continuing consultation is likely to be misinterpreted and the funds misdirected in their use. Furthermore, the persons representative of the consultative and administrative machinery must have the kind of status which engenders confidence and security. The development of machinery as outlined here would provide the confidence required both at the giving and the receiving ends, and is more likely to reassure individual institutions of the wisdom of accepting corporate responsibility for major projects.

In so far as Anglo-American co-operation is advisable and necessary in any particular instance, the existence of a United States Universities Advisory Council working in the manner suggested would make for easier consultation and for confidence. In the event of Anglo-American joint sponsorship of any particular project being desirable, such sponsorship undertaken by Anglo-American universities would be better planned and be more acceptable if it were provided under the joint advice of the Inter-University Council and a United States Universities Advisory Council.

Such a procedure would reduce the risk of political suspicion. In this respect the establishment of the new university colleges under British auspices has been characterised by internationalism in the teaching appointments at all levels. This gave witness to the world-wide character of university learning and made the colleges something other than new government institutions. An institution whose expatriate staff dominates its counsels and teaching is much more likely to be accused of being ' imperialistic ' in its intentions if it is staffed entirely by nationals of the sponsoring nation than is an institution whose expatriate staff is truly international in character. In this respect the national differences between persons recruited from different parts of the Commonwealth have been advantageous. Despite common traditions, institutions have developed sufficient individuality of outlook for the differences to be recognisable to the students and to local persons having dealings with the new universities. The existence of these differences contributes to a sense of political neutrality about the institution and its purposes. This is probably more important for the students than for local politicians and administrators, for within ten to fifteen years from its inception a new college will have produced a significant number of alumni, most of whom, in the circumstances of the new nations, will be exercising an influence out of all proportion to their professional status when compared with the men and women of the same age and status in other countries.

This points to another matter to be considered, that of the continuity of personnel. Staff should be appointed for a sufficient period of time to ensure the growth of close personal relations between key persons within and without the college and between staff and students. Several problems are involved here, to which British experience has not provided the answers. American attitudes may possibly modify the significance of some of the problems.

In many of the territories where help is wanted the circumstances in which people live may appear to be inimical to family life. The majority of the recruits are either young people, not yet involved in bringing up children, or persons who have grown-up families and therefore are no longer concerned with educating them. In both categories the appointments tend to be of comparatively short duration. In addition, few people are likely to be attracted to long-term careers away from their homeland, and in almost every case there is bound to be some anxiety about the future both in terms of career opportunities and in terms of security. The latter has been provided, to some extent, by the extension of F.S.S.U. [1] facilities to the oversea colleges. The former has been a matter of goodwill. For the exceptionally able, goodwill and proved ability appear to be sufficient. But universities need a lot of good teachers who never hit the heights scholastically : for them the comparative isolation of oversea exile for a period of years results in anxiety about the future of their careers. The answer to this problem lies partly in planned programmes of secondment and partly in working out long-term co-operation between the old and the new institutions of higher education. There may be greater anxiety

---

[1] F.S.S.U. stands for Federated Scheme for Superannuation in Universities. This provides for joint contribution by employer and employee to a superannuation scheme.

in Britain than in America in this respect; but what is particularly emphasised here is that whatever the personal problems, the importance of reasonable continuity in the directing of research and teaching, with its effect on the growth, stability and influence of the new institutions, must be fully recognised and taken into account when planning undertakings of this kind.

One of the responsibilities that result from sponsoring university development is that of training local persons for appointment to the college. In this aspect of the work there are several considerations to be borne in mind. Once a man is appointed to the staff of a college he is likely to remain there, because there is no other institution of comparable status in the country to which he might move. Herein lies danger of growing inwards from which the university must be safeguarded. Any programme of staff training must include at least an initial period of advanced study and teaching elsewhere, and regular international contact. When a single university is responsible for sponsoring a new institution, protegées must be sent to institutions other than the parent one for advanced study and further experience. This provision of further training and experience and of continuing oversea contact will require much more money than is generally available even in the more generous university budgets, and it must be planned with due regard to local national needs and to resources in other professional and official fields.

Comment has already been made on the subject of equating qualifications as they affect recognition of the status of the individual. But it is a matter which also is of considerable importance in terms of institutional responsibility. One of the more valuable features of the scheme of special relationship between the post-war oversea university colleges and the University of London was the confidence that it gave the local people in their colleges. This confidence ensured that non-degree diplomas and certificates, introduced to meet special interim local needs (e.g. the Associateship course for experienced non-graduate teachers earmarked for posts of special responsibility), were accepted, and were not considered to be qualifications invented to fob off the people with an inferior article for local consumption. In this respect it is highly desirable that the first courses, offered in a new institution, in a territory where a university college already exists, should have the hall-mark of already recognised authenticity. The new university college in Eastern Nigeria might quite unwittingly be handicapped if anxiety to get teaching started resulted in establishing courses of an unfamiliar pattern. Whatever is attempted to meet urgent needs by courses that are unorthodox must be done with due regard to status and future developments. Only too frequently interim qualifications, reasonable in themselves for the circumstances they were devised to meet, have proved embarrassing to governments and frustrating to the individual recipients, because little or no thought was given to making the first qualification a recognised part of the normal qualification.

Whatever is done to deal with the need for interim qualifications and relating of them to future improvement of status, it is essential that the qualifications awarded be defined by the university in relation to the studies pursued rather than to the posts to be filled. In other words, it is for the employing authorities to define what they regard as qualifications for appointment quite apart from what the university defines as qualifications awarded for studies successfully pursued. Whereas, pre-1939, the Yaba Higher College non-graduate (in British terms) qualifications were a continual source of agitation because they were, in the eyes of all concerned, courses merely devised for the jobs, in Ghana the non-graduate courses were defined and recognised by all concerned as university courses leading to university qualifications of a specific kind. It is clearly recognised that these qualifications fit the possessor in certain respects for appointment to certain kinds of posts, but do not carry with them automatic right to a post. Clear distinction in these matters adds to the independence of all parties concerned, yet at the same time permits of the maximum of consultation and co-operation between the university and the government.

In all this the important thing is that the university must accept responsibility for meeting the needs of the moment, not as necessary evils, or part of the price to be paid for doing the things it wants to do, but as innovations to be built into the established pattern of university activity. Certificate and diploma courses must be seen in the context of research and learning as well as in terms of professional and vocational training. Courses leading to non-degree qualifications must not be treated as chores to be undertaken by the less well-qualified members of a department. This mistake has been made on occasion in the past, and has been a source of irritation that has contributed to unhappy relations between the university and government.

When a new institution of higher learning is set up under joint Anglo-American aegis, it is probably in the provision of courses of study of an interim nature, and in the provision of professional courses, that there will be greatest danger of misunderstanding. The British are more likely to find difficulty in accepting the provision of such courses as the duty of a university. They will probably be doubtful about standards and also about the appropriateness of the content to the university-level teaching. There is no short answer to this problem, but anxiety about and opposition to non-traditional courses can be alleviated to a considerable degree through acquaintance with practice elsewhere. This could be provided by planned exchange of British and American teachers. Valuable though short visits can be, and valuable though the contributing of special lectures by visitors can be, they do not result in the understanding that comes from sharing in the normal teaching and discussion that takes place in a department.

Another aspect of co-operation that needs to be given attention is the provision of further training for young African and Asian students, especially those who will take up teaching appointments. Whenever possible, the period of oversea training and experience ought to be planned to include comparable British and American experience, and the planning should be through consultations on a tri-partite basis and not concerned merely with ensuring that person A visits institution X in the U.S.A. and institution Y in the United Kingdom ; visits for study and observation, which have not been adequately prepared, frequently result in prejudiced comparisons and misunderstandings. The appropriate parallel or supplementary experience is often missed. At short notice it is sometimes difficult to discover what is really appropriate to the needs of the visiting student. Where the visit in the second country is fitted in at the last moment, a student may not succeed in getting in touch with the appropriate people. Successful planning in these matters requires detailed knowledge and experience, and close accord between British and American collaborators, as well as with the sending institution.[1]

[1] Reference may be appropriately made here to the newly established co-operative Afro-Anglo-American programme to strengthen teacher education in and for Africa in which the University of London Institute of Education, Teachers' College, Columbia University and six African Institutes and Departments of Education are to participate.

4

Partnership in Oversea Education

There is a story told of Richard Porson, that when, very tardily, he fulfilled the duty equivalent to that of giving an inaugural lecture, he did so in three brief sentences. Whether the story is authentic or, as I rather suspect, part of the Porsonian apocrypha makes little odds. What is probably regrettable is that it did not develop into a tradition, though I suspect, for many, if not for most professors, to produce an inaugural lecture in three brief Porsonian sentences would be a trial to be faced with greater trepidation than is the existing conventional requirement.

The office which I now hold, and which requires me to give this lecture, is defined as ' Professor of Education with special reference to education in tropical areas '. In some respects this is a misnomer in that the latter part of the definition, in my opinion, ought now to be ' with special reference to education in the New Nations or the Emergent Nations '. If such a change of title were made, it would reflect the latest change in the political character of the field of study of education which was inaugurated in the University of London Institute of Education during the 1920s under the inspiration of James Fairgrieve and which gave rise to the establishment of the Colonial Department in the Institute.

Colonial Department, Tropical Areas, New Nations. In these three labels we have, as it were, some indication of the elements of past and current experience and of future aspiration essential to every successful educational endeavour, and it is in something of these terms I wish to attempt a partial review and forecast of our particular field of study.

In 1925, as a result of Christian mission thinking under the

64

leadership of Mr J. H. Oldham, American generosity in the guise of the Phelps-Stokes Commission reports on *Education in Africa*, a constructive attitude on the part of the Imperial government and the willing concurrence of the Colonial governments, there was brought into being an Advisory Committee on Education in British Tropical Africa which within a few years became the Advisory Committee on Education in the Colonies. That body, initially under the joint guidance of Mr A. I. Mayhew and Major Hanns Vischer as Advisers, and in succession to them Sir Christopher Cox, enunciated policy and offered advice in a series of memoranda and reports which set the pattern for educational development in British tropical areas with an authority and purposefulness of direction that previously had not existed. The Imperial Conferences on Education held prior to 1914 showed some recognition of education as a matter of government concern but did not provide an instrument for systematic and continuing oversight of policy. Under the influence of the advice provided by the Advisory Committee the Colonial territories proceeded to develop educational facilities by their best lights and within the limits of the resources available to them.

The emphasis that was thereby laid upon the importance of education in the development of the colonial dependencies made new demands upon the mission organisations who previously had been, and at that time still were, the chief providers of educational facilities. It also resulted in the expansion of, and in some cases the initial provision of, government education departments. What previously had been on the part of the Christian missions an activity subordinate to their main duty, of witness to the Word of God, became a major responsibility requiring considerable professional service. Similarly, for the governments, a negligible or minor administrative duty became the work of a major department requiring the services of professional specialists. The Colonial Department of the Institute of Education was a direct response to this need, providing facilities for training recruits to mission and colonial government educational services, accumulating source material for research and investigation, and stimulating thought and practice in the field of study.

In the first memorandum [1] produced by the Advisory Committee the concept of co-operation was laid down as a fundamental guiding principle. While the government reserved to itself the right to direct educational policy and to supervise all educational institutions by inspection or other means, it desired that voluntary effort should be encouraged and Advisory Boards of Education should be established in each dependency to ensure the active co-operation of all concerned.

This concept of partnership was evident not only in the colonial territories. It was a feature also of the Advisory Committee itself, which included, in addition to the representatives of the mission and government interests, representatives of educational interests in Britain of the highest calibre. In the Colonial Department of the Institute of Education the factor of partnership was to be seen in the sharing of the facilities for training and study by mission and government recruits as well as by small but significant numbers of students from the dependent territories. It was also demonstrated through participation in the teaching of the Department by Mr Arthur Mayhew and Major Hanns Vischer, and through mission workers and colonial government education officers on furlough sharing their experience with the new recruits in training.

The elements of partnership as between the missions and the governments in the making of policy and its practical application and as between the university, missions and governments in training and research had their counterpart within the university itself. An Institute of Education established in London primarily to provide facilities for professional training for men and women intending to enter the teaching profession in Britain was not equipped to provide facilities for the study of African or Oriental languages, nor was it equipped to provide the sociological and anthropological background knowledge and outlook necessary to the relating of the content and method of education to the local circumstances of the oversea territories. Co-operation between

[1] *Educational Policy in British Tropical Africa*, Cmd. 2374, H.M.S.O., 1925

the Institute of Education, the School of Oriental and African Studies and the London School of Economics provided the answer to the immediate needs and served to emphasise the inter-relations between the different fields of studies.

Throughout the thirties and the early forties (during the latter, despite the impact of the war) progress towards the provision of adequate systems of education in the several territories proceeded at varying pace, with local variations in priority and phasing of development, and differing degrees of appreciation of community needs in respect of social, economic and political circumstances. If experiments in adaptation, such as the Malangali School attempt at using traditional tribal training in discipline and citizenship, the attempt in Sierra Leone to introduce modern health instruction into the traditional initiation training of women, and the Omu School experiment in Nigeria, had proved inconclusive, the importance of education as a social institution involving the whole community, young and old, had become clearly established, and its significance to political, social and economic progress accepted by all. This was expressed explicitly in the Advisory Committee report on Mass Education in 1944 in these words : ' A man may be healthy though illiterate. He may be prosperous without being learned. He may, while still almost entirely ignorant of the wider duties of a citizen, live and, indeed, enjoy life under a government which provides him with security and justice. All these things may in a measure be true, but it is far truer that the general health of the whole community, its general well-being and prosperity, can only be secured and maintained if the whole mass of the people has a real share in education and some understanding of its meaning and its purpose. It is equally true that without such general share in education and such understanding true democracy cannot function, and the rising hope of self-government will inevitably suffer frustration.' [1]

There is one further backward look which it is necessary for us to take. In 1945 two Royal Commissions and a sub-committee of one of them completed the exposition of policy in advisory

[1] *Mass Education in African Society*, Col. No. 186, H.M.S.O., 1943

terms with a general report on higher education in the colonies, a report on the higher education needs special to the West Indies, and a report on higher education in British West Africa. If there were cynics who saw in these particular commissions further examples of the Royal Commission device being used as an instrument for procrastination they must have been rudely surprised. For, in a remarkably short period of time, new university institutions were established in all the territories and an exercise of partnership in education of a new dimension came into being.

This new demonstration of partnership contains two features deserving particular attention. In order that the institutions should receive the best advice and assistance possible, there was brought into being an Inter-University Council for Higher Education in the Colonies, representative of all the home universities and each colonial university or college. Through this instrument the Secretary of State was provided with the best possible sources of advice on academic aspects of any scheme for which financial aid might be sought from Britain, and the colonial institutions were provided with an authoritative source of advice on any matters of academic policy if they so desired it. The other new feature of partnership was the creation of the scheme of special relationship between the colonial university institutions and the University of London, whereby in the initial stages the students of the new institutions might be awarded degrees of the University of London, the latter body maintaining standards whilst providing for syllabuses to be adjusted to local conditions and giving the staffs of the new institutions experience of teaching and examining to an accepted university standard.

Despite strictures passed by a person so eminently qualified to comment as is Dr K. Mellanby, whose apologia for his stewardship of the early years of University College, Ibadan recently published under the title *The Founding of Nigeria's University*, is as enlightening as it is readable, the genius of this particular exercise of partnership in education has been clearly demonstrated and promises even more far-reaching consequences for the future. As for the scheme of special relationship between

68

the University of London and the oversea institutions, if I may be permitted to offer a personal comment after benefiting for nine years as a member of a junior partner in the scheme, I trust that now, having become a member of the senior partner to the scheme, I may be able to give in as goodly a measure as previously I received.

What all this amounts to is that over a period of less than four decades, in a variety of territories mostly but not all of them in tropical areas, there have been developed systems providing formal education of a comprehensive character together with less formal educational facilities for adult community education relevant to local needs and circumstances. In the process there has been demonstrated a spirit of co-operation and partnership of an exceptional nature. This partnership, I would suggest, derived its strength from the existence of a specific goal, which at the moment of apparent achievement implies new opportunities for partnership.

The goal was first described by Lord Macaulay on 10 July 1833 in a speech delivered to the House of Commons on the subject of the government of India when he said : ' It may be that the public mind of India may expand under our system till it has outgrown that system ; that by good government we may educate our subjects into a capacity for better government ; but having become instructed in European knowledge they may, in some future age, demand European institutions. Whether such a day will ever come I know not. But never will I attempt to avert or retard it. Whenever it comes, it will be the proudest day in English history. To have found a great people sunk in the lowest depths of slavery and superstition, to have so ruled them so as to have made them desirous and capable of all the privileges of citizens, would indeed be a title to glory all our own.' [1]

This is an end that has frequently been in doubt in the eyes of many dependent peoples, and the wisdom of the end is still

---

[1] Lord Macaulay, Government of India: A Speech delivered to the House of Commons on 10 July, 1833. Macaulay: *Prose and Poetry*, edited by G. M. Young, Hart-Davis, 1952.

questioned by some of our countrymen intimately concerned with dependent communities, and this despite the unequivocal expression of the objective made one hundred and ten years after Macaulay when the responsibility of the Imperial government for the dependent peoples was stated to be to ' secure (i) the improvement of the health and living conditions of the people, (ii) the improvement of their well-being in the economic sphere, (iii) the development of political institutions and political power until the day arrives when the people can become effectively self-governing.' [1]

What we are now concerned with is education among nations embarked upon a venture, as yet unproved ; with hopes set upon communities in which men shall be given unchecked control of their own lives.

It would appear that to a great extent the partnerships of the last forty years must of necessity largely disappear. The direct participation of the Christian missions in education appear to be giving way to participation being shared between the indigenous churches, local and national authorities. The colonial educational service is giving way to local national educational services. The development of Institutes and Departments of Education as concomitants of the new university institutions points to local provision of academic and professional training previously supplied by the home universities. But these features of change are appropriate parts of the process of development implying the change and development of roles rather than mere replacement and disappearance of some of the actors.

The faith evinced by the people of the new nations in education as the keystone to their national and individual futures is already resulting in an expansion of educational facilities far beyond present local manpower resources, and will continue so for many years ahead ; and there are clear indications that far more men and women will be needed to assist in the development of the expanding systems than can be trained for the purpose through existing facilities. This does not mean, however, that the continuance of the existing facilities or their

[1] *Mass Education in African Society*, Col. No. 186, H.M.S.O., 1943

expansion in their present form is the sole responsibility ahead of us. Rather, it means the discovery of the areas of training and research which will represent the appropriate element of special contribution to be made, as for example in 1944 it was recognised that the provision of special facilities of study for trained experienced non-graduate teachers ear-marked for posts of special responsibility was an appropriate special contribution in the then existing conditions.

If a venture at prophecy is permissible on such an occasion as this, then it may be suggested that among our primary contributions in the immediate future may well be the provision of special facilities for study and reflection for those men and women, whatever their previous training and experience, who find themselves, as senior members of their local education services, responsible for providing professional advice to their political masters and responsible for interpreting in a satisfactory professional fashion the educational aspirations of the people they serve. Such professional interpretation calls for imagination purged and judgment ripened by ' awareness of the slow, hesitant, wayward course of human life, its failures, its successes, but its indomitable will to endure '.[1] Such purging of imagination and ripening of judgment may more easily be recognised, if not come by, in this country where we are involved in an educational experiment based upon an exceptional accumulation of experience and knowledge and subject to a strength and wisdom such as is attainable only as we are able to stand on the shoulders of those who have gone before.

The political leaders of the new nations are particularly prone to the dangers of general suspicion and distrust, and stand in particular need of integrity of purpose in their professional advisers. If in the field of education those who accept professional responsibility for policy and its administration fail in open-mindedness and brave free discussion, then the communities they pretend to serve will rapidly find themselves on the slope which leads to aboriginal savagery and fratricide instead of

[1] Judge Learned Hand, ' The Future of Wisdom in America ', *Saturday Review*, 1952

climbing to the summit of civilised living in mutual confidence. In this respect some words of Marc Bloch are not inappropriate for our consideration, words which he committed to paper in 1940.

> The duty of reconstructing our country will not fall on the shoulders of my generation. . . . France of the new springtime must be the creation of the young. . . . It would be impertinent on my part to outline a programme for them. They will search for the laws of the future in the intimacy of their heads and of their hearts. The map of the future will be drawn as a result of the lessons they have learned. All I beg of them is that they shall avoid the dry in-humanity of systems which, from rancour or from pride, set themselves to rule the mass of their countrymen without providing them with adequate instruction, without being in communion with them.[1]

To provide opportunity for the educational leaders of the new nations to so equip themselves that they will provide adequate instruction for the mass of their countrymen and to remain in communion with them is a responsibility that requires the re-examination of the content and methodology of education in the circumstances of the new nations, with the most careful attention to the current social, political and economic facts against the authentic heritage of their own past as well as those elements of our own heritage which they choose to integrate into their own future tradition.

The re-examination of the content and methodology will involve, among other matters, consideration of the place and purpose of the teaching of languages, science, religion, the arts and the social studies.

In all the nations with which we are concerned we find to a greater or lesser degree a multilingual situation of a complex of languages and dialects and great disparities in the development of written form. In many instances, despite the labours of the small body of linguists who have devoted themselves to the study of the languages, little is yet known of their structure, usage or potential future value. The failure on the part of

[1] Marc Bloch, *Strange Defeat*, O.U.P., 1949

educational workers to investigate and experiment in their use as media of instruction, and ambiguity in attention to, and in interpretation of language policy, has on occasion led to abuse of the apparatus of linguistic study and of the results of the findings of such studies. A further complication has been the result of vested interests giving rise to the intrusion of distracting emotional factors providing fuel for pseudo-psychological theorising and lending strength to neo-tribalism masquerading as nationalism. To establish in a satisfactory manner the place, content and treatment of language in the education of the young of the new nations will call for the widest degree of co-operation between educationalists, linguists, anthropologists and sociologists in circumstances where matters of personal prestige and face are reduced to a minimum significance.

If the ignorance, which his critics in their hindsight accuse Macaulay of, when castigating him for his famous or infamous minute of 2 February 1835 is put in proper perspective, it can still be said of English with a permissible degree of literary licence that, ' whoever knows that language has ready access to all the best intellectual wealth, which all the wisest nations of the earth have created '.[1] It is likely that political independence will result eventually in a lowering of the emotional significance of local tongues and the development of a more objective appreciation of the essential necessity of learning English as an international language, and as the key to economic and technological know-how freed from the suspicion of devious imperialistic significance. Valuable as has been the past study of the teaching of English as a second language, in the future it is likely to become of much greater importance.

At a time when the most powerful nations of the world are planning to invade other solar bodies and close observation for other galaxies is likely to become a matter of serious theorising it would appear unnecessary to suggest that the place of science instruction is a matter needing special attention. But the circumstances of the new nations are such that attention to the

[1] Lord Macaulay, Indian Education Minute of 2 February, 1835, Macaulay: *Prose and Poetry*, edited G. M. Young, Hart-Davis, 1952

content and treatment of science in the schools is particularly urgent. The jump from ancient concepts of the physical world as they exist in Africa and Asia may, in some respects, be easier than the jump from the world of Dalton and Newton to the world of Rutherford and Einstein, but it is a jump that would the more easily be made if its nature was better understood. Another reason for paying special attention to the place of science in the school curriculum of the new nations arises from the fact that so little development of the teaching of science has as yet taken place that there is much more scope for experiment in the teaching of the subject as part of the general equipment of the layman as a citizen-to-be and in the preparation of the potential specialist and technologist. A third consideration arises from the fact that to all intents and purposes the communities with whom we are concerned have yet to move from a peasant to a technological way of life. The process of by-passing the experience of Europe and America, even the by-passing of the briefer experience of Japan and Russia, in this respect, sets problems and offers opportunity deserving our attention.

A fourth consideration is the contribution of science to health education. It was demonstrated during the First World War that knowledge of the facts governing health did not necessarily result in sound health practices either individually or co-operatively. We are a long way yet from the provision of satisfactory programmes of health education, and in the schools we have much to learn from the experiences of mass education and community development experience about both the content and the teaching of satisfactory health attitudes and practices.

In view of the major part that the Christian missions have played in education in the areas we are concerned with, it is a matter of surprise that so little originality has been shown in the study of the content and treatment of religious instruction. Part of the failure is, without doubt, due to the conservative theological outlook of the evangelical movement and the equally strong conservatism of the teaching profession. In part, also, ignorance concerning indigenous religions, written off as barbaric and antagonistic to the one true faith, has contributed to the

74

absence of experiment in a study, subject more than any other subject to the control of established dogma. Furthermore, as has been the case generally in education in the oversea territories, there has been a lack of dissemination of information about the few experiments in content and method that have been attempted.

In all the communities we are interested in the religious situation is complex. In Africa, Christianity and Islam are intrusive faiths established in varying strengths on an animistic substrata. In Asia other ancient religions hold their sway. The teacher, in whatever circumstances he teaches, should have understanding and sympathy of these religious influences in the life of the community as a whole and in the lives of the individual pupils for whom he is responsible. This alone sets a problem in education that will not lightly be resolved.

In the related field of education for citizenship the impact of modern ideas and practices upon older traditions set problems of content and method in geography, history, moral instruction and character training that cannot be met adequately merely by taking over and superficially adapting the solutions that have been worked out in circumstances unrelated to the ways of life and thought of the new nations. The solutions are to be sought by bringing to bear upon the problems exact knowledge of the ways of life the peoples are developing in the changing circumstances. It is more than unlikely that the school will fail the community in preparing the young for the responsibilities of citizenship if this is regarded as merely a matter of pedagogy. It is a matter in which careful prescription of content and ingenuity of invention in techniques of instruction will count for nothing if there is absence of understanding of the objectives. All of which suggests that the point of responsibility, initially at least, is to be found in teacher education. In this, as in religious education, we are involved as partners in receiving as well as in giving. Satisfactory solutions to the needs of the new nations in religious education and training for citizenship will provide us with material, and possibly teaching techniques, to help to provide our own children with a better understanding of the other peoples as members of the world community.

In communities whose economic resources are under-developed or largely limited to primary products the anxiety for vocational education tends to be overstressed. Together with sociological undertones, such as the assumed necessity for preventing the drift from the land and the assumed importance of teaching the dignity of labour, these considerations have led to disappointing experiments that have served but to underline the need for educational planning to be related to economic trends if the planning is to prove constructive. The prospects of agricultural and technical development that are held out by such agencies as the Colombo Plan, Commonwealth and United States economic aid projects, and the like, are setting new educational problems that will require the harnessing of the best resources in a co-operative effort if frustration and misery is to be avoided. Furthermore, political independence, resulting in local communities becoming directly responsible for their own corporate and individual well-being, is already creating a different climate of opinion about agriculture and technology, and thereby is opening up the way to a re-appraisal of the function of the education system in respect of vocational training.

The place of the creative arts in the curriculum at all levels of formal education leaves much to be desired. Despite brilliant work by isolated individuals in music and in the visual arts much of what passes for art instruction is but imitative repetition of the most uninspired practice still current in Britain. Local arts and crafts, in so far as they are introduced into the classroom, with brave exceptions, are treated without understanding of the nature of their roots in indigenous life. Furthermore, there is a ' museum-complex ' about much that is attempted. The first requirements, in this respect, would appear to be the establishment of the nature of local aesthetics, and of the creative significance of the arts as part of the curriculum. These are things that probably will not be done satisfactorily until African, Asian, Caribbean and Polynesian artists and teachers are able to integrate the traditional significances of their arts with the purposes of education as they are developed and expressed in the schools. This is a process that calls for patience and imagination, insight and sympathy, as well as exceptional teaching ability.

Underlying all formal instruction should be a thorough knowledge of the individual as an individual person and as a member of society, the knowledge of which we seek through sociological and psychological studies. To record that such social and psychological instruction as is provided in the teacher-training colleges in the territories we are concerned with is still almost entirely an imported product, frequently without even the misleading but superficially satisfying coating of local illustration of the accepted British or American exposition of theory, is but to say that the necessary research and investigations have not yet been carried out to the extent that makes it possible to integrate the findings into the training of the teachers. That this has not yet come to pass reflects the lack of the specialists and the lack of facilities for the systematic and persistent pursuit of the necessary studies. It also reflects the slowness with which the profession has come to appreciate the importance of these studies to daily classroom practice.

Now it may be accepted that what I have described as the kinds of thing to which study and investigation should be devoted are properly deserving of current attention, but it can be argued that most of them are matters that can be dealt with satisfactorily only in the field, that London is not the place for the pursuit of such studies, and that furthermore the existence in the new universities of Institutes and Departments of Education provides the most satisfactory facilities for the pursuit of such studies. To such argument I would reply that it is true that there are now existing in most of the areas with which we are concerned Institutes and Departments of Education, and that it is true the field work cannot be pursued in London. But I would point out that the existing Institutes and Departments of Education are very small ; their local resources are limited. In many cases there is a greater accumulation of knowledge, and may I dare say it, even of wisdom, in London than is available at any one of the new institutions. For these reasons there is a continuing responsibility on this University to provide partnership in the study and promotion of education in the new nations.

There is also, I would suggest, a special duty, in this field of study, as in so many others, that London is peculiarly fitted to provide, namely, that of a clearing house of information and as a central exchange of opinion and ideas. It would be easy to provide examples of unnecessarily duplicated effort, of mistakes repeated through lack of information of individual effort in different but parallel educational situations.

The urgency with which educational workers are being pressed by political leaders of the new nations for working answers to current needs leaves far too little margin of time for the educational workers to digest and disseminate the findings of their studies. Anxiety on the part of political leaders to make progress, to obtain results that will commend themselves to their voters and to justify their policies, is likely to increase the pressure and further reduce the possibility of the standing back which is essential for the long view ahead. Here is something that can be provided by partnership between the old and the new foundations, provided in part by the advantageous apartness of geographical circumstances enjoyed by the old foundations from the more immediate tasks, provided in part by the possibility of exchange of workers.

Nor should sight be lost of the importance of the partnership being a matter of mutual advantage. Some reference has already been made to this implication in the relationship. Two further brief references may serve to underline it. In 1944 plans were prepared for intensive and systematic attacks upon illiteracy in the dependent territories. Teaching people to read and write led on to what has become known as community development, revealing new possibilities of adult community education from which we might well be able to learn something to our own advantage. Secondly, the prospect of large-scale and comprehensive psychological and sociological studies now possible among the new nations as a result of facilities for research being made available in the new institutions, may well reveal facets of study and application obscured from us by familiarity with the

78

ways of our own community. Approaching the study of educational development among the new nations in the correct manner must be to our mutual advantage.

There remains one aspect of the partnership upon which I wish to comment. I referred at the beginning of the lecture to the fact that there was an element of American participation in what I suggested was a crucial step forward for education in the then British colonial dependencies. I refer to the contribution of the Phelps-Stokes Commission. Since then American philanthropy through the Christian missions and through the sponsorship of the great trusts of Carnegie, Rockefeller and Ford, and the Fulbright scheme have contributed increasingly to educational endeavour in the new nations. There have been, and there still are people, sometimes influential persons, who suspect such American endeavour as being an expression of dollar imperialism. Such prejudice is without foundation and is detrimental to the establishment of a united world community. The tide of educational endeavour will eventually wash away such prejudice. Meanwhile the co-operation which has existed in the past in this field of education must be strengthened and extended. The educational needs of the new nations are such that the maximum of efficiency of effort is essential. That efficiency of effort will be attained if as in the past we see the responsibility for the study and extension of education in the new nations as an exercise in partnership.

My discourse has departed very far from the suggested ideal of three Porsonian sentences, yet there is much unsaid.

May I end on a personal note. Having served my student-apprenticeship in this place under James Fairgrieve and Dr Mumford, my period as a lecturer-journeyman in this same place in the company of Professor Margaret Read and Mr A. S. Harrison, I count myself the most fortunate of men to have been able to return here to profess my subject under our Director, Mr Lionel Elvin, my immediate predecessor in office.

5

The British Contribution to Education in Africa

Why should an attempt be made, at the present time, to review the British contribution to education in Africa? What is the nature of that contribution? What lessons are there to be learnt from reflection on that contribution? These are the questions that I shall attempt to answer.

To many people an examination of what is past and done with is a sterile academic exercise, or, at best, is but the maundering privilege of old age. And to many people Britain is perhaps in her old age. Certainly direct British responsibility in Africa will shortly be a thing of the past. At the present time too, indirect assistance is being rejected by Africans who, impatient to be done with all signs and symbols of imperial tutelage, are looking in other directions for inspiration and help. Friends and enemies alike are rushing in at breakneck speed, sure of their ability to do better. On the face of it then, there are sufficient reasons to regard the British contribution as ended. It is true that direct responsibility is being given up. But we cannot irresponsibly withdraw support from a situation of which we have unique knowledge and experience. We, therefore, have a continuing indirect responsibility, all the more onerous and difficult to discharge, because assistance and co-operation will have to be given in conditions sometimes tinged with suspicion and impatience. In these circumstances a review of the work done in the past is timely. But even more important than this is the fact that, whilst education is essentially concerned with the immediate present and the future, it is rooted in the past. The significance of this emerges in the writings of many educationists, three of whom I wish to quote as being particularly apt to our theme.

Firstly, an American contemporary, Robert Ulich of Harvard University :

> We are fumbling around in education because we know so little about the future and do not bother to know enough about the past. Education is not only one of the greatest human enterprises in immediate planning with parents, teachers, ' educators ', school administrators and college presidents as its leaders. It is also a long enduring process of cultural self-evolution. This process expresses itself through the minds of men who are interested in, and capable of, looking deeper into the nature, the needs, and the aspirations of human beings than are most people.
>
> As long as the daily planning, doing and structuring in education are constantly nourished by the wellspring of the total cultural evolution, education and civilisation are in a state of health, when contact is cut they are sick and a crisis occurs.
>
> We live now in such a crisis. The degree of futile busy-ness constantly increases in proportion to the loss of a feeling for cultural depth and continuity.

In Africa at the present moment, under the exciting stimulus of political change and because the facilities for education are rapidly being expanded, there is little sense of ' futile busy-ness '. Many educators in Europe and America are confused in their values and are not sure where the emphasis should lie today. In this country the debate about the Crowther report is evidence of the bewilderment. In the United States of America the discussion about the merits of liberal and special education is evidence of the confusion that exists. Whatever bewilderment there may be about educational purposes in Britain or America, in Africa the dominating concern is for expansion. But the very busy-ness about speeding up the expansion of the provision for education may blind people to the real crisis. This crisis is one which Africa shares with the rest of the world, and is the same kind of crisis as concerned Comenius and his generation in seventeenth-century Europe. Professor Campagnac described

81

the situation and the attitude of Comenius in words that deserve
to be kept in mind :

> Comenius was a good, simple man. He lived in a troubled world :
> there were wars and rumours of wars, old rules of conduct and
> forms of belief were threatened or broken ; men were at once
> uplifted and bewildered by new knowledge which they did not
> know how to relate to what their fathers had known and frightened
> by new dangers, against which they seem to have inherited no
> safeguards nor could invent any. Instead of strife he wanted
> peace ; instead of confusion, order ; he wanted to test new things
> by truth tried and proven ; old beliefs he wanted to enlarge and
> reinterpret by using new discoveries ; with growth, to control and
> direct it, he wanted a principle of unity. He wanted to make an
> intelligible whole of life and the world. He wanted a way of life.
>
> That is what all men want, whether their lot is cast in pleasant
> or rough places.

Nearly three hundred years ago Comenius strove to find
satisfactory educational answers to problems fundamentally the
same as those we have been tackling in Africa, a task yet to be
completed. This is more than sufficient reason for looking
back.

Thirdly, may I draw your attention to some words of
Dr Margaret Read, the distinguished first occupant of the Chair
of Education with special reference to education in tropical areas,
in the University of London :

> In colonial education we are dealing with a historical process which
> began on a certain date, and has certain defined and recognisable
> stages which follow one another chronologically. It is surely of
> the first importance that there should be a history of education,
> conceived and carried out in the best objective traditions of his-
> torical research and presentation, for each colonial territory, to be
> used by those who are planning education and the teachers who are
> carrying it out. In this historical survey the initial impetus and
> motives for introducing ' Western ' education, as well as the
> agencies by which it was introduced, need making clear. The
> successive systems of education from the initial start up to the

present time should be traced, whether under voluntary agencies or the state, or a combination of both. The process of welding together diverse systems into an administrative whole can be studied in educational codes and ordinances, including as it does establishment of financial provision on an increasing scale. It should be possible too, through an examination of reports, speeches and legislative debates, to get some idea, even though an incomplete one, of the ideology held at different stages in educational development by those who were responsible for its planning and practice. . . . The present crisis is in itself sufficient reason for a historical study of educational achievements in the past. . . . If we can achieve these histories of educational development . . . we shall at least have a firm basis of facts. The need for this equipment, of an objective and indisputable character, is the more important when we come to look at other general considerations, which have been grouped under the . . . headings, political, ideological and cultural.

In brief, what does all this add up to ? Education without reference to the well-springs of cultural evolution is an unhealthy institution. The radical changes now taking place in Africa call for extraordinary foresight. Foresight is impossible without hindsight, and this in Africa calls for careful study of the work of British educationists.

We might for a moment consider who these people were that made the British contribution to education in Africa. They are a great variety of men and women : missionaries, government officials, merchant traders and private persons from all parts of the United Kingdom. And, what perhaps is not fully appreciated, many Africans who, having accepted the British way of life and thought have striven to pass it on to their fellow Africans. The first of these devoted and remarkable African educators to whom I wish to refer is Philip Quaque of the Gold Coast. Sent to England by Thomas Thompson, the first English missionary to Africa in modern times, Philip Quaque for fifty years after his return to Africa taught his own people, and the school he founded has continued in existence until this day. Then there was Edward Blyden, of Liberian origin, who worked and agitated for education in Sierra Leone. His conduct at times must have been irritating to his mentors, and at times possibly smelled of sedition. A third African specially deserving mention is Henry Carr of Nigeria, whose appreciation and understanding of the British traditions, and whose consistent service to education in Nigeria has yet to receive from his own people the credit it deserves. Incidentally, it may be worth recording that in the dark days of the last war when it appeared that Germany might overrun North Africa, Henry Carr was less concerned with the immediate outcome of events than he was with the possibility that for a second time in the century Britain might sacrifice the flower of her youth, a sacrifice which he thought would be a tragic loss to Africa and the world.

Then there is that group of African men and women who, on their own initiative and with their own resources, established schools when neither missionary nor government help was forthcoming. Such efforts derived their inspiration from the British tradition. They are as much part of the British contribution to education in Africa as are the contributions of such distinguished governors as Sir Gordon Guggisberg and Lord Lugard, and of such missionaries and educationists as Frazer of Achimota and Laws of Livingstonia.

It would be fascinating to tell the story of the work of the individual men and women, but it would inevitably result in neglect of another group of people, those men and women who, in the tradition of the British Civil Service, have made their contribution anonymously. It is a tradition that has obvious political merit and in the widest sense is being accepted by the Africans who have taken over from the British Civil Servants. But it is a tradition that has its defects, not least that whilst the errors and mistakes are not excused nor covered by the cloak of anonymity, successful and distinctive contributions too frequently do not receive due acknowledgment.

The work done by all these people, missionaries, government officials and private individuals, is to be seen in schools and colleges that now exist all over Africa. But of much greater importance is the work they did in establishing a policy and creating systems of education in the different territories, through which the policy could be implemented.

Turning first to the systems of education we note that the initial efforts were made by private persons with two quite separate purposes in mind. The first was evangelistic. Missionaries wanted to present the word of God to the people as the key to salvation, and so taught them to read the Bible. The second purpose, to train local workers, derived from the needs of traders, missionaries and government officials. The major need was for men able to read and write and to keep accounts. These purposes emphasised the importance of intellectual skills as evinced by book learning. Many contemporary critics have condemned the early attempts at providing schooling as being too bookish and unrelated to the needs of the people. Bookishness there was and still is, but there was and still is much relevance in the bookishness. And, it should also be remembered, that from the start attention was given to teaching practical skills. Crafts and agriculture have featured continually in the education programmes. Frequently the efforts in these directions failed, for reasons that were not easily recognised or particularly susceptible to diagnosis and treatment. Those who are critical of these past efforts might with advantage turn to an examination of the causes of failure. The experience would be salutary.

The move from private endeavour to public responsibility was a slow one. This is a long story, involving issues of administrative responsibility that I do not propose to pursue here. But it is worth remembering that as early as 1882, when British responsibility in Africa was still tenuous, an Inspector of Schools for West Africa was appointed by the government. In 1911 an Imperial Educational Conference foreshadowed the interest in African education in Westminster that was to come to fruition twelve years later in 1923 with the establishment of the Advisory Committee for Education in Africa, a few years later to become the Advisory Committee on Education in the Colonies. The establishment of this committee was a major step forward and was the beginning of a new phase for education in Africa. For, quite apart from the work it has done, it showed education to be the joint responsibility of government, voluntary agencies and the local people. It came into being as a result of consultation between the Imperial and the local colonial governments and the missionaries concerned with education.

The first major task undertaken by the Advisory Committee was that of defining the principles that should guide the making of educational policy. The memorandum in which the statement was made was published in 1925. It was based upon consultations between the interested parties already participating in education in Africa, and drew upon the best available experience in education in Britain. Furthermore, full use was made of an American offer of co-operation in the form of the Phelps-Stokes commissions on education in Africa. This was an act of enlightened statesmenship that proved of inestimable value in the preparatory study of the educational needs of Africa. The ready acceptance of American experience and generosity have been a consistent feature of British practice in Africa throughout the present century.

The statement of principles made in 1925 still deserves attention. It provides a yardstick by which to measure what has been done and, what is more important, still provides a basic guide to what is necessary.

In summary the principles then laid down were :

1 While the government reserved to itself the right to direct educational policy and to supervise all educational institutions by inspection or other means, voluntary effort was encouraged and it was suggested that Advisory Boards of Education should be established in each dependency to ensure the active co-operation of all concerned.

2 Education should be adapted to local conditions in such a manner as would enable it to conserve all sound elements in the local traditions and the social organisations, while also functioning as an instrument of progress and change.

3 Religious training and moral instruction should be regarded as fundamental to the development of a sound education, and

in the schools these subjects should be accorded complete equality with secular subjects.

4 The development of African dependencies on the material and economic side demanded a corresponding advance in expenditure on education, and, in order to realise the ideals of education it would be necessary to attract the services of the best available men and women. To do this the status and conditions of service would have to be satisfactory.

The rest of the memorandum dealt more specifically with matters reflecting considerations of organisation and administration.

5 Schools run by voluntary agencies which attained a satisfactory standard of efficiency should be regarded as of equal importance in the scheme of education as schools directly organised by the government, and should be given grants-in-aid. The conditions under which grants-in-aid were given should not be dependent upon examination results.

6 The establishment of a sound system of education was dependent on a sufficient supply of trained teachers, and the teacher-training institutions should be guided by the principles of education laid down in the memorandum.

7 A cadre of visiting teachers should be established to ensure inspection and encouragement for the teachers in village schools.

8 Thorough supervision was indispensable, and inspectors should seek to make the educational aims clear and offer friendly advice and supervise their own schools in ways parallel to and co-ordinated with the government system of inspection.

9 Technical and vocational training should be carried out with the help of the government departments concerned and under their supervision. Belief in the dignity of manual work should be encouraged and efforts should be made to promote equality of status with clerical service.

10 The education of women and girls should be treated as an integral part of the whole educational system.

11   Systems should be established which, although varying with local conditions, would provide elementary education of several types, technical and vocational education, institutions of higher education which might eventually develop into universities.

This is an aspect of the subject to which I will return. Finally, the need for some form of adult education which would ensure identity of outlook between the newly educated generation and their parents is noted. These principles, first enumerated in 1925, are, in my opinion, still valid, application of them being a matter of adjustment to changing circumstances.

In the years that followed a succession of documents was produced. Some of them were consequential upon the detailed consideration of particular aspects of education referred to in the 1925 memorandum. Other documents were produced dealing in detail with such matters as language and science teaching, and training in citizenship. In 1935 detailed attention was given to the need to relate the work of formal education to the circumstances of the local communities, the results being made available in a *Memorandum on Education of African Communities*. In 1944 it was the turn of adult education to receive special attention, the outcome of which was the *Memorandum on Mass Education in African Society*. As a result of this report steps were taken to develop mass literary work, and to encourage the people to work together using their own resources, make roads, build local health and community centres, improve water supplies and expand food production. In other words the report provided the initial statement of policy for what we are now calling community development.

In 1945 the reports of the Royal Commission on Higher Education in the Colonies spelt out the details of the programme for higher education. This resulted in the establishing of university institutions, and colleges of arts, science and technology, in East and West Africa as well as in Asia and the Caribbean. Although the establishment of institutions for higher education was included in the recommendations of the 1925

88

memorandum to which I have already referred, the scale on which the development of university education has taken place since 1945 was certainly not envisaged. Decisions recently made to expand the provision for higher education in East Africa, and the recommendations of the Ashby Commission for Nigeria, are but the latest demonstrations of the British concern for education in Africa.

Statements of policy and programmes, however, are one thing ; what matters to most people are the practical outcomes. Looked at in terms of statistics, the picture is patchy and some aspects of the picture are extremely depressing. In every territory there is a shortage of adequately trained teachers, the education of women and girls continues to lag behind that of men and boys, the number of illiterates is still so high that effective communication between the governments and their peoples is frequently difficult if not impossible.

Estimating the school population to be one-fifth of the total population, we find that the number of children not in schools is still very great. In the secondary schools there are not enough places for all who are capable of benefiting from the opportunity for secondary education. Of even more concern at the present time, such provision as exists is quite inadequate to meet the demand for persons with secondary education. The facilities for higher education also fall far short of what is desirable. Humbling to our self-esteem as these figures may be, in themselves they can be very misleading, for they do not reveal either the total dimension of the task involved or the economic difficulties inherent in the situation.

The amounts of money being spent may appear to be very meagre by comparison with expenditure on education in affluent industrial societies. But it is not from lack of concern for education that this is so. In this respect it may be wise to remind ourselves that the first grant-in-aids for education in Africa were made by Parliament at Westminster in 1809 when money for education was included in the establishment vote for Sierra Leone, before Parliament had accepted any responsibility for spending money on education in Britain. That did not come about until 1833. Critics of the amount of money spent on education in Africa in the past too frequently base their judgments on a valuation of education which is, in fact, of very recent origin.

It is often suggested that the British contribution to education in Africa has always been too little and too late. Measured in material terms this undoubtedly has an element of truth in it, but it is a judgment that savours of wisdom after the event. This is even more true of the strictures made about much of the content of education. It is easy to poke fun at the rigid adherence to curricula and syllabuses used in English and, not infrequently, Scottish schools, and to deride the slavish acceptance of the English examination systems. Two things should be kept in mind, however. In the first place people had to start with what they knew and were limited by their own educational experience. It is much more difficult to adjust and adapt, or invent new material to meet new circumstances, than the observers on the side lines generally realise. The need for adjusting, modifying and inventing, both in terms of the content and methods of education, was recognised and indeed enunciated as a principle early on. Attempts were made at Malangali in East Africa and at Omu in West Africa to use local traditional ways of inculcating discipline and of training character in schools, to mention but two imaginative attempts at relating the work of the schools to local conditions and needs. The fate of these and similar experiments serves to underline the difficulties of the policy of adaptation. Furthermore, if the use and development of African languages and literature have proved disappointing it is not from lack of thought or effort but is the consequence of the intractible nature of the work to be done. Review of British attempts at relating the content and methods of education to local needs suggests that their greatest value lies in the variety of solutions that have been attempted, and in the persistence shown in pursuing this policy rather than in the degree of success attained in specific experiments. That it is the only policy to follow is unquestionable, but it will never be an easy one to work out in detail.

Success in relating the content of education to the local conditions is, of course, dependent upon knowledge of the local environment. This fact was recognised by the men and women who were responsible for founding the new university colleges in Africa. For them the problem was related to another of equal importance, the one of ensuring that the standards of the new institutions should be generally accepted as adequate. The solution to these inter-related problems was sought through the scheme of special relationship between the new university colleges in Africa and the University of London. Whilst the University of London had final responsibility for the assessment of standards, the local university teachers were given every encouragement to relate the content of their teaching to the local environment.

The syllabuses they produced have attracted criticism. But careful examination of research that has been carried out and of the way in which the results have been incorporated in the teaching suggests that creditable efforts have been made to adapt the work to local conditions.

Furthermore, scrutiny of the current autumn lists of the university and commercial publishers suggests that we are reaching the point at which the studies of the last ten years in the new-university colleges are influencing the content of the textbooks for use in the schools.

That this has happened so quickly reflects credit on all concerned with the work. And I wish to emphasise—all concerned. The original studies that have produced the new knowledge have, of course, been the work of the local university scholars. But they are indebted to the support they have received from the universities in the United Kingdom channelled through the Inter-University Council for Higher Education Overseas, and to the support that has come from government officials in this country and in the African territories. The latter, though much less publicised, is just as important as the former.

It may not be inappropriate at this point to utter a word of warning. The urge to expand the facilities for university education, political ambitions and to some extent political opportunism may lead governments to press for changes in the control of the university colleges and in the kinds of courses they provide. Impatience with the present provisions may lead to hurried modifications and experiment. These will be necessary, of course, but too rapid and too frequent indulgence in change is likely to result in harm rather than good.

It is exceedingly difficult to judge correctly at what stage to embark upon a major change or step forward in education. There was a timeliness about the steps taken by Britain to provide for higher education in Africa that is specially significant. Having due regard to the social and economic conditions, I would hazard the judgment, that World War II apart, an earlier major effort would have been premature and a later one could have been tragic.

The timeliness of the British contribution to higher education in Africa was not accidental. It was due to the policy of continuing review carried out by the colonial governments and by Whitehall concurrently, the views of those concerned with day-to-day responsibilities being balanced by the views of the more detached observers at Whitehall. Outside observers do not always understand this feature of the British system, whilst the ' man on the spot ' has the ultimate responsibility for decision, his judgment is guided by the opinions of men and women of wide experience in Britain as well as by the more immediate reactions of the local people. Such a balance of counsel, systematically provided, has its own continuing value.

Outstanding among the many contributions made by Britain to education in Africa was the systematic formulation of principles to guide the establishment and the development of an education system. Even more important has been the presentation of the concept of education as a social institution, fundamental to the healthy political, social and economic growth of a community. This concept has been expressed in many ways. Guggisberg gave expression to it in words that have become a slogan : Education, the Keystone. More recently, the role of the British Government in respect of Africa was defined by the *Memorandum on Mass Education in African Society* as the securing of :

(i) the improvement of the health and living conditions of the people ;

(ii) the improvement of their well-being in the economic sphere ;

(iii) the development of political institutions and political power until the day arrives when the people can become effectively self-governing.

The part that education plays in achieving these aims was described in the following terms :

A man may be healthy though illiterate. He may still be prosperous without being learned. He may, while still almost entirely ignorant of the wider duties of a citizen, live and, indeed, enjoy life under a government which provides him with security and justice. All these things may, in a measure, be true, but it is far truer that the general health of the whole community, its general well-being and prosperity, can only be secured and maintained if the whole mass of the people has a real share in education and has some understanding of its meaning and its purpose. It is equally true that without such general share in education and such understanding, true democracy cannot function, and the rising hope of self-government will inevitably suffer frustration.

In those two statements, namely, the definition of the political objectives of British rule in Africa, and the description of the significance of education in the fulfilment of the objectives, we have a measure of the worth of the educational effort.

What then are the essential features of the British contribution to education in Africa ?

I suggest that in essence British educationists have (i) provided a set of principles to serve as a guide in the building of an education system ; (ii) laid the foundations for such a system ; and (iii) offered a concept of education as a social force whereby it becomes the means of creating a socially, economically and politically healthy society.

Much remains to be done. This is a fact not to be hidden and ignored but to be freely admitted. In this admission lies the incentive for further effort. The principles that have been formulated, however, will remain sound guides for those who will be responsible for education in Africa in the future.

And what of the lessons to be learnt from reflection upon the British contribution to education in Africa ? The first lesson is the importance of recognising that education is fundamental to the social, economic and political well-being of a community. Unfortunately, in considering the financial consequences British policy was handicapped for many years by the fact that the education departments were regarded as spending departments and were not provided with the money necessary for them to make their full contribution to social and political development.

The second lesson is that the people as a whole must understand and accept the value of education and be willing to share fully in its provision. Consultation was recognised as an important principle in formulating educational policies, a principle applied mainly to those professionally engaged in educational work. Little attempt was made to inform the general public or to engage lay opinion in discussion of educational policy. In consequence the people have not been as fully concerned with education as they ought to have been.

There is a third important lesson to be learnt from the history of British educational effort in Africa, an aspect that I have hitherto not touched upon. It is the danger of allowing considerations of political expediency to modify educational planning. Twice in the last century the accumulation of educational experience has been largely dissipated because political considerations overshadowed all others. In the 1920s the need to economise on government expenditure because of the slump resulted in the wholesale discharge of education officers. Again, in recent years, the abrupt termination of the appointments of experienced education officers, as well as those of other experienced colonial servants, following the granting of independence, has resulted in a loss of experienced man-power, the effects of which are likely to be felt for many years to come. There are other examples of political decisions adversely affecting educational development that could be quoted. The lesson to be learnt is that what may appear to be minor set-backs to educational work almost invariably result in cumulative ill-effects.

There are many aspects of the British contribution to education in Africa that I have not attempted to examine. It must, however, be remembered that apart from the provision of education through schools and colleges in Africa there has been a constant stream of Africans to schools and colleges and to industries in this country. The Press, the B.B.C., the British Council, the Armed Forces all have contributed directly or indirectly to African education. Their importance is not easy to assess, but to ignore their part would be to distort the picture.

Whatever assessment is made of the British contribution to education in Africa, it cannot be gainsaid that there has been much solid achievement and that sound foundations have been laid. Undoubtedly some features of the work have been unsatisfactory. But the best measure of its merit lies in the determination of Africans to extend the provision of education as rapidly as is possible. Remember, they are the products of the education system they have inherited.

What of the future?

The people of Africa will have to forego other things they want so that every available penny is invested in education. Even this will not be enough. Countries outside Africa will have to help with men and money. In what must for many years be an international exercise, Britain has a special contribution to make from its past experience in Africa as well as from its historical heritage. In this respect it is to be regretted that the British Government has not seen the way clear to establishing a Commonwealth Education Service, which could ensure the kind of continuity that has marked the past work of Church and State in education in Africa.

6

Education and Social Growth

Principal, ladies and gentlemen, I address you this evening under the constraining consciousness of two dicta. The one I will refer to now. If time remains at the end of the lecture I will make reference to the other. For the moment I am constrained by the knowledge that as Saintsbury remarked in 1920 ;

> Most plain men would agree vaguely—and not a few who have some special knowledge of the subject would agree scornfully or mournfully, according to temperament—with Peacock's more than fifty-years-old dictum that the nonsense talked on education would outweigh all the nonsenses talked on any other subject.

Be that as it may, I propose to consider in this lecture the future of education with reference to the interaction between formal education and the changing social structure of the people of the Gold Coast, or as the world will shortly be recognising it, the Ghana nation.

There is nothing new in this approach. Education is the process by which men acquire the civilisation of the past, are enabled to take part in the civilisation of the present and contribute to the civilisation of the future. The necessity for the process arises from the nature of man who, at birth, is not equipped for life but with capacities that enable him to live. The manner in which these capacities may be developed is dependent upon the outlook on life possessed by those who undertake the responsibility of educating the young, and that in turn reflects the outlook of the society to which both teacher and taught belong.

96

In daily practice these things are taken for granted. Discussion of educational matters is usually determined by the need for settling issues calling for more or less immediate action, and assumptions are made about the social and political framework without critical examination of their validity. With a nation entering upon a new era, however, it may be deemed proper to suggest that it is timely to examine some of the ideas underlying educational practice. To do so is to enter upon a procedure that will certainly be difficult, and may well be dangerous. In the time at my disposal I must of necessity generalise. Furthermore, the matters at issue are such that prejudice and emotion can easily creep in. Such matters are best dealt with by stating them explicitly and giving them as concrete an expression as is possible.

Briefly, my thesis is this. The people of the Gold Coast have entered upon a new phase of social growth. Emerging from a period of political dependency, which gave an artificial unity to a group of peoples of diverse origins, languages and loyalties, and entering upon a state of independent nationhood, the social and political situation is one of great fluidity. This fluidity is the more complicated because the peoples concerned are moving from a state of subsistence economy to a state of cash economy; from a peasant way of life to one which is at least partly urban. The concept of the family in its traditional extended pattern is being obtruded upon by a growing sense of personal individualism. Political authority within the tribal organisation with its emphasis upon the accumulated wisdom of elders is being challenged by the claims of the individual to independence of judgment based upon professional knowledge and the mass acceptance of party political programmes. Decision by agreement arrived at by the process of extended discussion and reflection, typical of the older tribal pattern of government, is being replaced by a reliance on the weight of numbers and is open to the evils of crowd emotion and demagogy.

Overlying this complex of fluid factors is the influence of a parentalism, political and religious, exercised by the Colonial government, which sought on the one hand to protect the people from past evils and abuses, real and assumed, and on the other hand to cushion them from too sudden impact with the complexities of the western world.

The situation is the more complicated in that the whole world is in a state of confusion. There are wars and rumours of war. Old rules of conduct and forms of belief are threatened or broken; men are at once uplifted and bewildered by new knowledge which they do not know how to relate to what their fathers had known; they are frightened by new dangers, against which they seem to have inherited no safeguards, nor can they invent any. It is a state of affairs to which Matthew Arnold gave expression in the concluding lines of the poem *Dover Beach* :

> The Sea of Faith
> Was once, too, at the full, and round earth's shore
> Lay like the folds of a bright girdle furl'd.
> But now I only hear
> Its melancholy, long, withdrawing roar,
> Retreating, to the breath
> Of the night-wind, down the vast edges drear
> And naked shingles of the world.
>
> Ah, love, let us be true
> To one another ! for the world, which seems
> To lie before us like a land of dreams,
> So various, so beautiful, so new,
> Hath really neither joy, nor love, nor light,
> Nor certitude, nor peace, nor help for pain,
> And we are here as on a darkling plain
> Swept with confused alarms of struggle and flight,
> Where ignorant armies clash by night.

Those who have held the responsibility of government both here and in the Imperial capital have in frequent utterances paid attention to this complex of changing conditions, and in their policies have shown recognition of the fact that the process of education has a fundamental part to play in procuring adequate adjustments to the changing circumstances. This belief in the importance of national educational policy as a determinant of the present and future social structure has in recent years been given increasing emphasis in educational writing, and to some extent has been pursued to an extreme which ignores the fact that education is not the architectonic science but is subordinate to that of politics.

In fact, the aims and purpose of the teacher are determined by the statesman. In a society in which the teacher, as a citizen, shares with other citizens in deciding what form of society is most desirable, the teacher shares in the responsibility of statesmanship in a dual form, as a citizen and as a specialist. In a society in which the subordination of the teacher to the State is determined by a dictator the educator is reduced to a menial tool in the hands of the dictator. The depth to which this may drive the teacher is reflected in the views of Hitler as recorded in *Mein Kampf*:

> The State that is grounded on the racial principle and is alive to the significance of this truth will first of all have to base its educational work not on the mere imparting of knowledge but rather on physical training and development of healthy bodies. The cultivation of the intellectual faculties comes only in the second place. . . . Formal education in the sciences must be considered last in importance . . . the State which is grounded on the racial idea must start with the principle that a person whose formal education in the sciences is relatively small but who is physically sound and robust . . . is a more useful member of the national community than a weakling who is scholarly and refined.

If such a picture is disconcerting, that which is presented by developments in the United States, equally reflecting the influence of political and social influences on education, is in some ways more insidious. Robert Hutchins has recently drawn attention to certain tendencies which have developed in American education.

> A student at Ohio University may now obtain a degree for learning how to be a news photographer. There is a Department of Mortuary Science at Wayne University in Detroit. When I mentioned this fact to a great industrialist in that city, he instantly

99

replied, 'Well, we need morticians, don't we?' So firmly is it ingrained in the American mind that whatever the community needs, or whatever a young person thinks he needs for his life work, can and should be taught in universities. On one day an industrialist will announce that it is the duty of the schools to teach that 'profit' is an honourable word. On the same day the Board of Regents of New York State says that the schools should devote frequent periods to teaching the country's moral and spiritual heritage. A little later a New York judge proposes to cure juvenile delinquency through a four-year course in the city's high schools on marriage and parenthood. We have come a long way since the declaration of the Yale faculty in 1829 : 'There are many things important to be known, which are not taught in colleges, because they may be learned anywhere.'

A third illustration of the subordinate place of education to politics is to be seen in the English Education Act of 1944 which was designed to make education a decisive process in changing the form of society. In the words of the Act,

> it shall be the duty of the local education authority for every area, so far as their powers extend, to contribute towards the spiritual, moral, mental, and physical development of the community by securing that efficient education throughout those stages shall be available to meet the needs of the population of the area.

The Act assigned to the State a new authority over education in that it empowered a minister

> to promote the education of the people of England and Wales and the progressive development of institutions devoted to that purpose, and to secure the effective execution by local authorities, under control and direction of the national policy for providing a varied and comprehensive service in every area.

Here, in the Gold Coast, the education system has been developed under the influence of Christian missionary effort, the deliberations of the Advisory Committee on Education in the Colonies as interpreted by the Education Department and local individual assessment of the needs and opportunities. Until 1941, when the Central Advisory Committee was set up, the community exercised practically no influence on the content or the system of education, despite the fact that on different occasions a considerable element of local interest had been shown in the idea of providing formal education on a Western pattern, and that individual Africans, concerned with the contribution to be made to the development of society through education, have expounded their ideas in newspaper articles and pamphlets and speeches.

The great change in this situation took place during the period 1941–50. One expression of it was seen in the springing up of schools under local stimulus without reference to, or direction from, either missionary or government authorities. It is this phenomenon which gave authority to that portion of the policy laid down in the Accelerated Development Plan for Education, 1951, namely, the aim to provide as soon as possible a six-year basic primary course for all children at public expense. The success in mobilising public opinion against the acceptance of the minority view of the Elliot Report, approved by the Secretary of State, which led to the passing of the Ordinance of the Gold Coast Government for the foundation of the University College of the Gold Coast on 11 August 1948, is another reflection of the political direction which underlies educational effort.

There can be little doubt that the interest in, and the willingness to support the development of, education that has been shown by the people, is due to the acceptance of the idea that education is the keystone of a people's life and happiness. The kind of education which will be sought will be determined by the values, political, social and economic that the community as a whole develops. So much is said in the foreword to the Development Plan for Education, 1951 :

A progressive modern educational system is necessarily a complex structure, for it must needs meet the many needs and aspirations of the nation as a whole and it must also care for the individual. . . . One of the most urgent needs of a progressive, democratic country such as ours is a measure of education (as much as we have the means to provide) for every child of school-going age. . . .

There is an urgent need, also, for much more extensive provision for secondary education. We need men and women with secondary education in many positions of responsibility in the Civil Service and in many other services. We need, also, a great reinforcement of students for the University College and for the Kumasi College of Technology. From these institutions of our own, and from places of learning abroad, we look for many men and women trained to the highest level to take leading positions in the whole life of the country. We expect from them devoted service to the betterment of the life of the whole country. . . . I have said enough to show that our government regards education as the key to our people's progress. Our country has great aspirations and it is determined to fulfil them. I am confident that whatever sacrifices may prove necessary will be willingly made for the great purpose of lifting our country to the highest standards of the democratic way of life.

Enough has been said, I trust, to show the relationship which exists between education and social growth. As far as the people of the Gold Coast are concerned there are certain postulates underlying the policy enunciated in the development programme which call for examination. The first of these is the postuatle that the right to an education is one of the fundamental human rights. The second postulate is that human mentality is multi-dimensional. The first of these postulates is generally interpreted to mean that every individual has a right to an education, and the meaning of the second postulate is ignored. The consequences of this thinking are dubious at the present time and if persisted in can become dangerous for the future. Education is not a commodity to be received from the hands of a benevolent community and passively received. Education, in fact, is not possible unless there is a living response and co-operation from the recipient.

The right that does exist is the right to such opportunities and aid as the mental capacities of the individual qualify him to use and stimulate him to take the trouble to use. This necessitates not only the provision of opportunity but also the recognition of the multi-dimensional character of human mentality. At present the practice is to estimate mentalities on a linear scale with the talent for scholarship being placed on the top. But the talent for ideas and abstractions which are essential for scholarship represents but one line of mental power. There are other mental powers. Central to the genius of leadership is intuitive perception of the controlling factors of complex situations, coupled with sympathy and love for men and sagacity in judging character. Biological pressures during adolescence cause rapid and extensive differentiation in taste. In some individuals the taste for adult life is sublimated through interest in the world of ideas, in others the pressures result in a reaction against study and lead to an extra-development of athletic, social or sexual interests, impatience for political action, or early desires for business or professional activity. The linear assessment of mental ability which dominates the education system carries with it the connotation of inferiority for the non-scholarly mental types, and contributes to a social differentiation antagonistic to that equality of respect which is a need of every individual and an essential for a truly democratic society.

The pertinence of this to the development of the education system begins with the process of selection for the opportunities available. Despite the studies that have been made of human abilities we are a long way from being able to ascertain what capacities are most significant in the individual. Our methods of examination are much more of the character of 'How much do you now know?' than of 'What do you want to know, and why?' If the selection process continues to be unsatisfactory the consequence will be that the education programme will prove inefficient in an economic sense, in that much time and money will be spent to no avail, and that an attitude towards education will develop which will expect not only facilities for education but the certificate of being an 'educated man' as of democratic right. Such an attitude will lead to a lowering of standards and a failure to produce men and women properly qualified to satisfy the needs and aspirations of the community.

It is necessary to develop satisfactory methods for assessing the actual and normal differentiations of mental powers. It is also necessary to recognise that over and above educational provision for scholarship, vocation and profession, there is the need for education of a general nature to fit all individuals for the career of citizenship. The first contribution to this will be made when the social distinction which exists between those who can read and write and those who cannot is eradicated. When this has been attained an immense advance towards the possibility of a working democracy will have been made. The way will then be clear for the providing of a genuine programme of general education, that is to say the educational equipment necessary for every individual to understand the civilisation to which he belongs and contribute to its maintenance and improvement. This calls for an examination of the content of the curriculum at the primary, secondary and post-secondary levels that needs to be lifted out of the field of immediate expediency, important though it is that we provide interim working solutions to satisfy the pressing needs of the moment.

One of the difficulties here lies in the misleading distinction made between ' useful ' and ' useless ' education. At the university level it results in a lack of co-ordination between the universities and the professional bodies. Where the universities have attempted to fulfil the dual role of teaching a subject as a branch of knowledge and of acting as professional schools, thereby attempting to be, in part, schools of theoretical instruction and, in part, vocational training establishments, they have fallen between two stools. Professional interests are for the most part so severely practical that in order to get a balance the universities tend to over-emphasise the theoretical. At the same time professional bodies tend to insist over-vigorously on the teaching of useful things. This dichotomy of interest is to be found throughout the education system except, possibly, in the earliest stages.

In any community parents exhibit anxiety about education fitting their children for earning their livelihood in the future. This frequently leads to the making of considerable sacrifices by the parents. It also leads to demands for education for employment. Vocational interests are pressed to the extent of jeopardising a balanced curriculum.

Here in the Gold Coast the most recent feature of this anxiety was demonstrated in respect of the former Standard VII school leaving examination. The attempt to do away with it foundered very largely because public opinion thought it necessary as a qualification for entry into paid employment. Other factors also contributed to the demand for its return. There were doubts about the efficiency of the teaching in the absence of the examination incentive, and also about the validity of assessments provided by the teachers of the level of attainment of the pupils. In this particular instance it is unquestionably true that public opinion, for a variety of reasons, was not prepared for a major change in educational policy. It is also true that the education authorities and their advisers were insufficiently appreciative of the social consequences of the change they advocated. Consequently they failed to provide a satisfactory substitute for the feature they wished to drop, and more seriously, failed to inform the general public of the advantages that might have been derived from the change. The result is that a growing item of expense is being added to the cost of education for many years to come, the possibility of developing a programme of cumulative records as a measure of attainment and ability has been indefinitely delayed, and the teaching profession has lost the incentive for exercising a more individual responsibility for the pupils in their charge. The machinery of educational administration is involved in providing two examinations for an age group when one or possibly none might be to the general advantage. Finally, the teaching, if not the content of the curriculum at the middle-school level, is likely for many years to be unduly influenced by examination requirements rather than by the best interests of the pupils and the community.

The problem illustrated by this particular situation is a dual one. It must first of all be established what educational process will best meet whatever are the needs of assessment at this particular age level, and, secondly, how the community as a whole can be led to appreciate what is best and thereby ask for it ?

Asking for any kind of educational programme raises an economic question which is recognised in the statement of policy accompanying the development programme :

> One of the most urgent needs of a progressive, democratic country such as ours is a measure of education (as much as we have the means to provide) for every child of school-going age. . . .

The action that was taken in 1951 to fulfil this obligation was essentially a political one, and in so far as it represented a genuine desire on the part of the great majority of the people it was a proper decision to make. The response on the part of the people as measured by the increase in the number of children who entered the schools is sufficient confirmation of the propriety of the decision. In December 1950 there were 204,262 children attending the primary and middle schools, in 1951 the number increased by 16,273. A year later, the first year of the application of the development programme, the number rose to 415,107.

The economic consequences of the decision were fully appreciated by those responsible for the administration of the exercise. In 1950 Mr T. Barton, in a lecture delivered in this college, indicated clearly the financial implications of the intended expansion, and whilst paying tribute to the contribution made by local authorities remarked :

> But the response from local authorities will have to increase. The prospects of that are greatly dependent upon the ordinary people understanding the necessity of paying their local taxes and seeing that their local taxation is giving a proper return in the provision of education. In all this the teaching profession has a dual responsibility, that of giving service to the community and that of establishing general community understanding of the implications of development in costs to the individual citizen.

The latter feature of this particular responsibility has not been fully realised by the teaching profession, nor for that matter by the administrative authorities. In consequence, the educational programme and those aspects where it is dependent upon local support has not fared as well as it might have in some districts.

Enough, I trust, has been said to indicate the interdependency of education and social growth. Some of the difficulties inherent in the present, and in the immediate future, are historical consequences of an education imposed as from above rather than emanating from the expressed desires of the society. Other difficulties owe their origin to the demand for action in respect of an immediate need. Yet other difficulties are the direct consequence of ignorance and misunderstanding.

The first requisite for developing an education system is undoubtedly the formulation of a widely comprehended definition of aims. This is dependent upon the society itself possessing a conscious appreciation of what kind of society it wishes to be. To claim that at the present time the Gold Coast is a progressive democratic country and that its education is directed to democratic interests is to beg the question. The Gold Coast is in fact a country which has chosen to model its future on a democratic pattern, and its educational system should therefore be developed in such a manner as to give every individual equality of opportunity. In doing so it will be necessary to exercise the principle of selection, selection with reference to abilities and with reference to differences between childhood, youth and age.

In terms of elementary education, it must be realised that it is not a finished product complete in itself but is a phase of growth. It must therefore be adequate to the tasks of childhood and be sufficiently forward-looking to prepare the individual for the tasks of adolescence. If the elements of primary education are accepted as ' the 3 Rs ', it must be remembered that the child is also a person and is not merely a reader, writer or doer of sums. The child has his own world to live in, a world which is shared by his elders. To provide a programme of instruction equal to the situation will require wise assessment of present needs and future opportunities. For many years to come, in the development of a curriculum and a methodology adequate to the task, it will be necessary to take cognisance of the fact that for a large proportion of the community the primary and middle school programme will represent the total opportunity for formal education. The temptation to overload the curriculum with reference to factual content, and the temptation to equip the child in respect of duties belonging to a more mature mental and psychological age level, will be great. These temptations will be avoided if the community as a whole appreciates that the child is ' father to the man ' and not the man in miniature.

The teaching profession can contribute to this general understanding if it equips itself with the tools of its trade, a process calling for sustained study of the child as a growing individual and as a member of a society of complex form, with rights and obligations as a member of an age group, a rural or urban community, possessing tribal and religious affiliations and belonging to a family. The collecting, assessing and interpreting of this data is a continuing affair, not to be contained within textbooks, but built up from persistent objective study of the living phenomena. It means that the teacher-to-be must be trained to think rather than to imitate, it also means that those teachers who show special capacity should have opportunity for advanced study in their fields of special interest ; a provision, however, that does not absolve any teacher from the responsibility of pursuing his own studies within the limits of his capacity. Furthermore, both the teacher and the non-teaching adult in society must understand and appreciate that the process of formal instruction provided by the State is but a part of the total educational process. Other contributions are being made, and will continue to be made, by the family, the religious institutions, the village or district group.

In the field of secondary and higher education the principle of selection is even more acute. In secondary education we are entirely imitative of a pattern derived from societies considerably different from that from which the Gold Coast is developing. It is a pattern that is undergoing considerable criticism in the countries of origin. We need to examine the purpose of the studies which, it is assumed, should be taught. The admission of any subject matter to the curriculum should be made dependent on the way and on the extent to which it puts the learner in possession of his cultural inheritance, enables him to enter into, and contribute to contemporary life and qualifies him for contributing to the future. The assessment must be made with respect to a number of terms of reference. The individual lives in a physical environment which controls him, and which he, in co-operation with his fellow men, can control. The individual is a member of the generality of mankind sharing in the heritage of its successes and failures and of its unfinished tasks. The individual shares to a greater or lesser degree a creative impulse, a talent to be cultivated and shared, not buried. Finally, the individual shares in the immensity of the universe and is involved in a process of values and ultimately of faith which finds expression in religion. The selecting of what shall be taught, and how, must be made with due regard to these criteria within the limits of the space and time available. It is even more important at this stage that the selection made is a matter of common understanding.

At the level of higher education the criteria governing the educational programme are complicated by the addition of the task of advancing knowledge. The teaching staff are scholars concerned with research, that is the extension of knowledge, as well as with teaching, that is the passing on of knowledge. A conflict of interest can and does occur where teaching and research tend to dominate each other. To separate them out into activities to be pursued in different institutions would be to lose in both fields of education. The claims of advanced professional training, referred to earlier, also exercise a complicating influence, and on occasion result in misunderstanding between the men of action in business, industry and politics and the men of learning. Complications of this character in a society such as the Gold Coast, which is passing through a period of rapid growth and change, call for the practice of the utmost degree of patience and consideration by all concerned if serious damage to the aspirations of the society as a whole is to be avoided.

We are at a point in the history of this country where the

framework of a system of formal education has been provided. The filling-in of that framework, and the equipping of all its parts, is to be carried out during a period when the people of the country will be evolving a new pattern of society with its own set of values, derivative in part from Africa, in part from the West and in part from a new world pattern that is painfully being evolved. The kind of filling-in, the equipment necessary and indeed the framework itself, will be much influenced by this period of vigorous social growth that lies ahead. Whatever form it finally takes, I would suggest that the general aim of education is as well described as may be in these words of J. L. Myers :

> To train the child first to appreciate what is going on in the natural world around him and among the members of society into which he is born, and second, to react intelligently to the situations and events, physical and social, as they occur in his life.

This necessarily involves training in self-knowledge, self-mastery and the habit of interpreting the actions of other people in the light of one's own feelings, desires and ideas. This is what Delphi meant when it said ' Know thyself ' and ' Nothing in excess ', and what Christ meant in the injunction to love one's neighbour as oneself.

The contribution that the teacher in the school can make is the justification for the existence of the schools, but it is not as significant as many people would suggest. A child is in school for only a small portion of his life, and even when he is of school age he is subject to the educating influence of the home and the community at large. This limited influence of the teacher was fully recognised by the Board of Education in England, when, in 1904, in defining the purpose of the public elementary school there was included this statement :

> And, though their opportunities are but brief, the teachers can yet do much to lay the foundations of conduct . . . implant in the children habits of industry, self-control and courageous perseverance . . . teach them to reverence what is noble . . . foster a

strong sense of duty, and instil in them that consideration and respect for others which must be the foundation of unselfishness and the true basis of all good manners.

Recognition in this fashion of the limitations on the teacher's influence, and recognition of the essential function of the teacher, emphasises the importance of the teacher's possessing a true sense of values about what should be attempted as well as possessing the knowledge of how best to attempt the task with each individual and with each generation. Seen in this light, the unity of purpose, content and method becomes clear. And much of the confusion that exists in educational thought and practice would be eradicated if the purposefulness was based upon a satisfactory set of values. This presents a challenge to the society as a whole, to those who administer education and to those who train the men and women who choose to serve that society through the vocation of teaching.

It is proper to ask of a university institution established for the furtherance of the process of formal education what exactly is the contribution that it proposes to make. The answer is given by the provision of courses of advanced training and study which involve attempts at interpreting values of society significant to the educational process—the study of principles ; by developing an understanding of the past with reference to its relevance to the present and the future—the history of educational thought and practice ; by experimenting in the fields of curriculum and method—methodology ; by relating the educational programme to the personal and social psychology of the individual as an individual personality as well as a member of society—the study of educational and social psychology ; and by co-operating with the Ministry of Education, local education authorities, the education units and all other organisations concerned with the process of education, general and vocational.

Some of these tasks are essentially matters of immediate action, others are matters involving patient and persistent study, influenced by the knowledge that a comparatively minor change brought about in primary school education in response to social or political pressure may have repercussions—the consequences of which may not appear until fifteen years or more later at the university level.

In all places and at all times the inter-relationship of education and social growth is a significant one. For the people of the Gold Coast the implications for the next two decades, or quarter century, are of exceptional importance. All who share in the responsibility, and that means the whole community and not just the members of the profession, must develop an increasing awareness of what is involved. The present faith in the value of education must be harnessed and constructively directed.

I have deliberately limited myself to a few facets of the formal apparatus of education in attempting to suggest the significance of recognising education as a practical science of subordinate, but at the same time of primary, use to the architectonic science of politics. Of as great importance are the informal and unorganised educational processes which proceed unceasingly through family life ; association with contemporaries of all ages, vocational activities, friendships, neighbourly contacts, institutional contacts of a religious, trade, professional and political character, and mass communication through the press, the camera and the microphone. In these respects the implications of social growth are much less appreciated than they ought to be. But that is matter for another occasion.

I opened this lecture by remarking that I was oppressed by two dicta. Whether the one I quoted at the beginning is relevant to this discourse will be for you to decide. The second one is much more easily proved and I trust I have not been a witness to its validity. ' A professor is one who talks in someone else's sleep ' !

7

Social and Cultural Problems of Urbanisation
for the Individual and the Family

Convention requires a speaker to express pleasure and appreciation at being invited to address his audience. It is a convention
that I comply with in all sincerity. Without the invitation, I
would probably have gone on being concerned in but a marginal
way with our subject as it impinges on my own field of interest.
The preparation of this paper has required my considering the
matter in much wider terms. I trust the results will be deserving
of your attention and a true measure of my thanks for the task
imposed upon me.

A transformation occurs when human societies change from
a rural form to an urban form because people previously living
in isolated circumstances, or belonging to societies with extremely
stable tradition, suddenly enter into the mainstream of world
activity and seek the material benefits of modern technology.
The move is to some extent freely motivated, but in every case
to a greater or lesser degree it is a direct consequence of the
intrusion of the West into previously isolated and relatively
stable societies.

The characteristic features of the transformation are :

1 previously isolated, self-sufficient rural economies are integrated into a single national economy with strong ties with
   world economy ;
2 the production of goods for personal use or direct exchange
   is replaced by or dominated by production for sale with the
   consequential emphasis upon a cash economy ;
3 technological processes based upon scientific knowledge are
   introduced into farming and manufacture and involve large
   measures of capital expenditure ;

4 complex and widespread means of communication and transport are developed ;
5 the division of labour and specialisation of occupations is intensified ; and
6 towns and cities grow through migration from the rural settlements.

Material development is dependent upon a fairly harmonious balance between these variables. When that harmony exists, the rate of change is modest and the impact of change on the individual and the family is a relatively slight one. Where, however, there is inbalance between these variables and where at the same time the rate of change, or of demanded change, is intense, the impact upon the individual is increased and results in great strain and tension. This, unfortunately, is the situation today in Asia, Africa, the Caribbean and South America.

The problems that arise are further complicated by the rate and manner of change in the political and the cultural spheres of human relations. Most of the countries now undergoing transformation from rural to urban societies are also undergoing, or have recently undergone, a change from a state of political tutelage to a state of indigenous political independence. This change is accompanied by a loss of the imperial administrative and professional leadership, and experience, at a time when the demands for experience and leadership are expanding and local experience is still limited. Furthermore, at the same time, the authority of, and the confidence in, traditional local indigenous leadership is being challenged and weakened, if not destroyed, by the political opportunism and the competence of the younger generation. This results in the reduction of the privileges of age, and in a questioning of the respect and deference traditionally given to the older person as the repository of the experience, knowledge and wisdom of the society. At the same time, the comparative rigidity of the system of priorities of seniority remains sufficiently entrenched to keep the young man waiting in his place on the escalator of advancement regardless of his skill and competence. Consequently special abilities are not fully used just at a critical point in development, and individual anxiety and frustration are engendered.

The existence of respect in young people for their elders is dependent upon the latter deserving respect. In the stable rural societies the old people are wise in the ways of farming, in the secular and the religious matters of the community that bear most heavily upon the individual. Control of the land, the most vital element in the life of the community, rests with the elders. In the newly established urban societies the migrant individual does not possess the knowledge, wisdom and authority relevant to the new situation. Children born to the migrant urban dweller quickly develop a far greater measure of understanding of the ways of life of the city. It is only when parents have established themselves satisfactorily in the earning structure of urban life and have developed a stable status that they take on the role of model for the children.

The values of the majority of the peoples now being subjected to this process of rapid urbanisation are in the main dependent upon religio-cultural systems such as animistic, Islamic, Hindu or Buddhist, all different from those of the West. In differing degree they emphasise spiritual rather than material values. After-life or future existences are of relatively greater importance than is present existence. The pressure to conform limits the significance of the individual, and within the family unit there is rigid definition of the role and status of the individual members. This definition of role is also exhibited to a greater or lesser degree in the village community and the wider social order. Ownership of property is expressed traditionally in non-productive forms, such as jewellery and cattle. Large amounts of energy and periods of time are given by tradition to social and religious rituals, ceremonies and festivals.

These value systems do not stimulate either the individual or the community to seek material gain for its own sake, nor do they encourage expectation of personal reward and advancement as a result of merit or persistence of application. In such circumstances a cash economy, work-leisure segmentation of time and employer-employee relationships are phenomena that lie outside the experience and comprehension of the migrant. Yet these latter are dominating features of urban life.

The problems for the individual and the family would be difficult enough were the societies homogeneous. But with few exceptions they are pluralistic. That is to say, they almost all contain exogenous population groups which have not been assimilated culturally, economically or politically. This is reflected in the cities in a number of ways. For instance there are generally great differences between the physical character of the Western-built city and that built by the indigenous population in their own tradition. The different ethnic and religious groups tend to create 'village' agglomerations within the city quite different from the segregation patterns of Western cities.

One other important general factor must be noted before turning our attention to the more specific aspects of change from rural to urban living and their effects on the individual and the family. It is the change in rate of population growth.

Increase of the rate of population growth is a phenomenon that has always accompanied the process of urbanisation. What makes it so important in present circumstances is the dimension of the growth as a result of a rapidly declining mortality rate accompanied by a continuing high or increasing reproductive rate. Whereas in Western countries it took periods varying from several decades to a century and more to halve the mortality rate, the countries we are now concerned with are achieving the same degree of diminution in something like a decade. In contrast there is no similar prospect of a similar rapid decrease in the reproductive rate.

In this respect the clash of cultural values and the time lag in the effective impact of the educational process are equally likely to slow up the adjustment of attitudes towards the number of children desirable and towards the means of controlling the number.

Quite apart from the importance of economics and food production there is another influence presenting a direct challenge to urban man who constantly expects more material benefits. Industry invents new luxuries, or produces bigger and better consumer goods. Advertising turns the novelties into ' necessities ', and they in turn become the measure of social status. Discrepancy between what people have and what they want, or think they are entitled to, increases frustration. The explosive population situation accompanying urbanisation presents moral problems of immense difficulty both to the individual and to the family.

Turning from the consideration of the general factors affecting the process of urbanisation to the contrast between rural and urban conditions, we find the rural situation characterised by strong settled traditions. Seventy per cent or more of the people live on farms and the surplus food resulting from their limited techniques permits of little industrialisation. Each community group tends to be self-sufficient in respect of most needs, and there is comparatively little trade or contact with the outside world. In an urbanised society as few as ten per cent of the people may be occupied in the production of food, thanks to the application of scientific methods : communications are widespread in character and permit of a high degree of mobility of persons and ideas.

In the initial stages of urbanisation there is a heavy flow of young people from the farm to the city. If the actual rural population remains stable the proportion of flow may be as high as three to one. In general there tends to be a slow growth of rural population in the early stages of development, but rationalisation of farm sizes and the adoption of scientific techniques reduce the possibilities of absorption of the farmer's children who of necessity must move to the cities.

The cities tend to be large and the human contacts tend to be in terms of specialised roles rather than between individuals as total personalities. Home, work-place, religious and social attachments are in essentially different places. Person-to-person relations tend to be limited and confined to particular purposes and rarely permit the development of total personal involvement. Social relationships are limited to the immediate family and a few ' close friends ', are based upon long personal contact and are essentially emotional in character. Money is the pervading determinant, affecting where people may live, what recreational facilities they may enjoy, what local community relationships may develop and what form of employment shall be sought with little concern for vocation or for the social value of the tasks undertaken.

Whilst urban life tends to weaken family and clan ties, and may result in great personal loneliness, the individual is involved in a complex of group relations which contrast strongly with the closed circle of rural family life. In rural circumstances the individual is a member of a single small group. All the important activities of his life are under the direct influence and scrutiny of the group. In the urban situation he is involved in a variety of groups, has a great measure of choice and can use the resources of one group to adjust or compensate for pressure within another group. Involvement is usually complex in variety but limited in scope.

In any urban community there are always a few rural migrants. In a rapidly growing centre the number of ' transitional individuals ' adjusting rural and urban conditions is very considerable. Such people tend to cling to those rural characteristics which are likely to provide a sense of security. This is particularly true of extended family relationships which may take on a clan or village character. On the other hand, many transitional individuals find the temptations and pressures of urban life tend to break the sanctions of rural society. The individual who finds himself a transitional character often comes to look down on his previous rural way of living as backward, uncivilised and old-fashioned. He finds himself imitating modes of behaviour he does not fully understand or appreciate. Occupational, religious, political and social associations take on new characteristics which fail to make an integrated pattern comparable to that of the rural community. The first generation transitional rural-urban individual generally finds himself in a precarious job with an income which provides little beyond the barest subsistence. Despite the new circumstances he finds it difficult to move far from his traditional culture. On the other hand, the loosening of family and tribal or clan ties and sanctions weakens the hold of traditional values and lack of education and knowledge limit his comprehension of the values and ways of the new order. With experience and education the individual may begin to find some kind of a pattern in the new ways. In general, however, the potential advantages of urban life are not fully grasped until the sons and daughters of the transitional generation enter into their inheritance.

The impact of urbanisation on the family is to be seen in the pressure in favour of the small closed family unit and against the more extended family unit characteristic of rural communities. The status and authority of the sexes and of the generations tend to become equalised, and the economic responsibilities of the family tend to be limited.

In the traditional rural community there is a strong sense of obligation to and dependence on the family. The individual shares things with the relatives, is secure within the family ties and responds to family discipline. Living in the same area, occupied co-operatively in common activities, subject to social controls of education, religious ceremonial and mental relations sanctioned by the family system there is little alternative, or, for that matter, concept of behaviour different than that traditional to the community.

The strength of these ties is such that the individual who leaves the rural community for the urban situation initially holds fast to the established values and relationships. The move, in original motivation, is almost always for the sake of the family, and may in intention be temporary. Frequently, however, the economic rewards fall short of expectation, and living in the town absorbs far greater a proportion of earnings than was expected. The duration of stay lengthens and new tastes and ties develop. During the early stages of transition the individual tends to lean very much on the strength of the family, and in some respects its authority and power may temporarily be increased. But as time passes the geographical separateness of members of the family and the expense of urban life coupled with the individualism of wage earning, result in a loosening of family obligations in their extended pattern and a strengthening

of the obligations to the more limited urban unit of his wife and
children. Dr Lucy Mair has provided a summary description
of this process in the following terms [1] :

> On the basis of the existing evidence it is possible to discern certain
> general trends. Many of these can be correlated with the general
> increase in freedom from control by personal authority which can
> be seen in every sphere of African life. This arises directly from
> the fact that the African village is no longer an almost isolated, self-
> contained world, within which each member is dependent on the
> good-will of the rest and must secure it by conformity with accepted
> rules, and which he cannot leave without considerable danger. The
> African of today depends for his material needs at least as much on
> sources of income outside the village as on the co-operation of his
> family and kinsmen, and colonial rule has established law and
> order which make it safe for him to leave his village, and means of
> communication which make it easy.
>
> One consequence of this situation is that marriage is becoming
> increasingly a matter of personal choice rather than an arrangement
> between groups in which the elders have a dominant say. . . .
>
> Where the marriage is made legal by a payment, the husband
> is coming more and more to be expected to provide this from his
> own resources . . . The substitution of cash for some or all the
> gifts or services included in the marriage formalities has often had
> the consequence of introducing a mercenary element that was not
> present in the old days. . . .
>
> The family found in the towns is usually the elementary family.
> Circumstances rarely make it possible for a wider group of kinsfolk
> to live in close contact. As a result, the influence of the ' family
> council ' in maintaining the stability of the marriage is weakened
> or even removed. There is no longer any organisation outside the
> family for inculcating accepted rules and values in the next genera-
> tion, and it is difficult for the family to meet this need when fathers
> as well as mothers have to earn money. . . .

Another commentator, Georges Forthomme, draws our attention to the effect upon the second generation of the changes of
family and clan ties consequential upon urbanisation [2] :

[1] 'African Marriage and Social Change', *Survey of African Marriage and
Family Life*, ed. Arthur Phillips, Oxford University Press, London, 1953, pp. 152–55
[2] *Mariage et Industrialisation*, 1957, p. 17

In the city, children grow up in groups that are not based on tribe or clan membership. Friendships are founded not only in the neighbourhood but also in school. A friend is chosen according to certain common interests, and becomes a person in whom one can confide, from whom one expects aid in times of difficulty. With him a helping hand is not so much an obligation but rather a sign of affection. When one can surround himself with such true friends, why sacrifice for a group that uses the tie of blood to put one at their mercy ? It is not just a question of an exchange of services with clan members, but the fact that the aid they usually demand is in the form of money, that thing so hard to obtain, which is lost once it is loaned to a relative.

Besides, the elders use the blood tie in order to impose their authority. But that right can be asserted only in the age-group that recognises it. That authority was justified formerly by all knowledge resulting from experience, but currently the occupational opportunities permit a young man to have a social role almost as important as that of an elder.

Such are the changing conceptions of those who are currently forming families. Although not excluding his parents, the modern young man primarily considers his family to be made up of his wife and children. Without doubt, he still hears the mystical voice of the clan : exogamy remains a vigorous principle, and one dares not break certain tabus, but the rules that were the base of the old social order appear old-fashioned and are progressively abandoned.

The native of the city, regardless of his tribe, is proud of his young independence which was won by work outside of the clan context. He no longer counts on the clan and if, in important decisions, he consults his father it is mainly a gesture of protocol for he expects his father's views to differ from his and he will follow his own inclinations. The cases of young people marrying against the wish of their parents is not rare.

The effect of urbanisation on the status of the woman is to give opportunities of greater independence. There is usually a shortage of women in the city and this establishes a market value, which is enhanced by the opportunities of independence through earning a living as a trader, domestic servant, office or store or factory worker. The opportunities of meeting other men when the husband is at work for fixed periods of the day provide alternatives for the dissatisfied woman and offer the opportunity of the ' profession ' of prostitution. Furthermore, the mixing of tribal and clan groups results in inter-marriage, thus increasing the possibilities of individual adaptation to new circumstances.

By way of contrast to the elements of family disorganisation and individual rebellion that appear to be a concomitant of much urbanisation taking place at the present time, the findings of Oscar Lewis in a study of the Tepoztecans living in Mexico City [1] (pp. 40–41) presents a somewhat different picture :

> We find that peasants in Mexico adapt to city life with far greater ease than do American farm families. There is little evidence of disorganisation and breakdown, of culture conflict, or of irreconcilable differences between generations . . . Family life remains strong in Mexico City. Family cohesiveness and extended family ties increase in the city, fewer cases of separation and divorce occur, no cases of abandoned mothers and children, no cases of persons living alone or of unrelated families living together.

By way of comment on the disparity of these findings from the general picture that we have of early phases of urbanisation, Joseph A. Kahl observes [2] that there were a number of special features about the situation. Tepotzlán is only two hours by bus from Mexico City, the urban dwellers visit the place frequently, and over half of them still own houses in the village. The Mexican rural family pattern is better adapted to urban needs than is the African. The Catholic religious traditions reinforce the family pattern and there is a general homogeneity of city population. He also points out that data recorded on disorganisation tends to be limited to problem features, thereby producing distortions of assessment of the total situation under review.

A recent study of industrialisation in Japan [3] also suggests

---

[1] *Urbanisation Without Breakdown: A Case Study*, 1952
[2] Joseph A. Kahl, ' Some Social Concomitants of Industrialization and Urbanization ', *Human Organization*, Vol. 18, No. 2, p. 68,
[3] *The Japanese Factory* by James C. Abegglen, Asia Publishing House. 1959

that social disorganisation need not necessarily be a consequence of urbanisation. The study brings out parallels between the factory system and the clan or kinship organisation :

> In terms of formal organisation some of these have included both the manner of recruitment into the system and the kinds of reciprocal obligations thereby incurred by company and worker. Further, the formal system of motivation and reward has functional parallels to that kind of kinship grouping. . . .
>
> Indeed, so pervasive are the parallels to a kinship-type organisation in the large Japanese factory that it is not necessary for the observer to argue their presence from indirect evidences. For example, in a 1952 speech to his managerial employees, the president of a large steel company said, ' Not only is there the fact that our life's work is our employment in our company, but I feel that as people in this situation we have two occasions that can be called a " birth ". The first is when we are born into the world as mewling infants. The second is when we all receive our commissions of adoption into the company. This is an event that has the same importance as our crying birth.' Here are both a direct statement of the kinship basis of company organisation and an indication of the way in which the common bond is symbolised, by treating the company, its history, and present organisation as an extended family with common values, common ancestors, and common beliefs. . . .
>
> It would seem from this study, then, that the very success of the Japanese experience with industrialisation may well have been a function of the fact that, far from undergoing a total revolution in social structure or social relationships, the hard core of Japan's system of social relationships remained intact, allowing an orderly transition to industrialisation continuous with her earlier social forms.

Commenting upon the implications of the Japanese experience in the problem of aiding the development of other non-Western nations, Dr Abegglen suggests (p. 105) :

> It would seem from the Japanese example that a considerable degree of tolerance—even at the cost of seeming waste—needs to be

allowed local custom and methods in establishing industry in those countries with systems of interpersonal relations markedly different from those of the West.

Complex as the problems of urbanisation are for the individual and the family in the town, they by no means represent the whole of the issue. For those who continue to live in the rural community there are problems of equal significance. These have tended to be obscured by a Western viewed concern for the assumed evils of the ' drift from the land ' . . . A concern that possibly has been emoted more by sentiment than by sense and knowledge. Discussing the subject of the current anxiety in India about what is described as the ' population explosion ', P. and P. Striet comment [1]:

> There are others, (factors which have a direct effect in increasing the desire for large families) however, that work to the same end, though in a much more subtle fashion. One of them is emigration. For more than a century Puri has been sending away its surplus young men—the boys who had they remained at home on the land, would have created acute population pressure. There has been a concerted village effort, in fact, to educate these boys and hence give them an edge over other job aspirants in distant areas.
>
> Today the sons and grandsons of Puri fathers can be found throughout India—as taxi drivers in Calcutta, as clerks in New Delhi, as mechanics in the new industrial complexes. Like many emigrants they have had a tendency to send some of their earnings home. It appears, therefore, that not only has emigration relieved the actual pressure of numbers that might have made the peasants curb the size of their families more than they have already done, but the cash received from distant sons contributes to their desire for more sons.

It is not unreasonable to suggest that more important perhaps than ' the drift from the land ' is the impact of the process on the individuals who stay in the rural situation or have not yet

[1] 'New Light on India's Large Worry', *The New York Times Magazine*, 13 March, 1960, p. 76

reached the stage when migration is possible. Indicative of the nature of this problem is a fifteen-year-old Japanese girl's composition about what she calls ' My Money Trouble ' [1]:

My composition is all about money, because I have not been thinking about anything else for a long time. I almost hate to go home because nearly every time I go, I have to ask mother for money for school. I thought I had paid for the school excursion, but found that I still owed three yen (less than a penny) for car fare. On the same day, I had to ask mother for ten yen and thirty sen (about three-pence) for my Natural Science textbook.

' It is all right,' said mother, as she gave me thirteen yen and fifty sen. ' I will give you what you need for your books, but you certainly do use a lot of money for school. Be sure to bring thirty sen change (less than a twentieth of a penny), for I have no small change.' I was relieved but my heart sank when my little sister asked for eighteen yen (about one shilling and fourpence) and mother began to scold. ' Your sister and brother have been asking for money for books and all sorts of things all morning, and I don't know what to do.' I hurried out, not wanting to hear any more.

When I got to school, I found the Treasurer and smilingly handed him the money. He counted it carefully and said, ' You owe for the Social Science textbook you got last spring.' Was it possible ? More money ? My heart sank again and I was no longer interested in anything our teacher said. What would mother say ?

After school, Soju was waiting for me. ' Bring twenty yen tomorrow for your deposit in the Pupils' Bank,' he said cheerfully.

Fourteen yen and twenty sen for the book and twenty yen for the Bank, thirty-four yen and twenty sen in all. What was I to do ? How could I ask mother for thirty-four yen and twenty sen ?

I wanted to stay at school and play, but I couldn't. I was so worried. ' When should I ask mother for the money ? What should I tell her ? ' I kept thinking about this all the way home, and I was so anxious about it that I could scarcely scrub the floor that afternoon. I tried to ask that day, but I simply couldn't. I

[1] *Echoes from a Mountain School*, ed. Seikyo Muchaku, tr. G. Caulfied and M. Kimura, Kenkyusha Ltd., Tokyo, 1953, pp. 23–28

tried to think of a good way to ask mother, but I simply couldn't tell her. She is always good about giving me money for school, but there are so many of us that it is hard for her to find enough money to get what we all need. It was not until I was ready to start for school the next morning that I said almost in a whisper,

' Mother, money for my Social Studies book and for the Pupils' Bank.' She couldn't understand what I said and turned to me. ' What did you say ? '

Important as the social and economic implications of the transformation from rural to urban are, in terms of values and institutions, even more important are the implications for the individuals in terms of their personal relations. This is probably the most difficult aspect of the process to assess and understand. The people responsible for the provision and the content of the schooling which the girl, just quoted, was undergoing, doubtlessly planned everything with the best of intentions and with full recognition of the function of the school in preparing the young for a richer and more fruitful life. That the kind of provision they had made was too demanding in personal terms on the individuals and the families might well come to them as a shock. Schooling is necessary. Competition for work opportunities makes it necessary for the rural school to provide all that the urban school does and more, but the rural community is less able to find the money. The imagination that can invent alternative solutions is a gift rarely to be found. The problems of tension and adjustment remain.

There is, as I have tried to indicate in this process of transformation, a variety of factors that exert influences on the individual and the family unit. These influences break the stable character of the traditional family. They encourage a reduction in the size of the recognised obligatory family unit, increase the freedom of the individual and give women greater opportunity of independence and equality. The younger generation has a wider choice of personal relationships and of career. But in the initial phases of urbanisation these changes involve culture shock, and the absence of institutionised forms of economic, social and cultural relations can result in bewilderment.

126

Where the rural community continues to exist, it in turn suffers stress and strain.

Understanding, and with it the capacity to deal with the problems, has been handicapped by lack of knowledge in detail ; research workers have been preoccupied with attempts to state trends in abstract terms instead of paying attention to the concrete facts in each situation. In addition, the assessments attempted have, for the most part, been Western-determined. This is to say, Western experience has been the basis of the viewpoint from which the problems have been examined. Furthermore, anxiety about the problems has possibly obscured some of the constructive and positive aspects of the process. Concern for these positive features could lead to more satisfactory interim ways of meeting disturbing negative features. The Mexican and Japanese studies that have been referred to indicate the value of paying attention to the specific situation, and also suggest that there may be important influences at work that we have been unaware of because our viewpoint is conditioned Western experience.

These considerations raise questions about the place of Christian thinking and activity. The Christian Church by the nature of its witness and by its participation in social activities has been a profound influence in stimulating social change. By the very nature of the Christian understanding of man and community the Christian as an individual and as a member of the institution of the Church is committed to working for a change in the character of human society. In the past much of the authority of the Church in missionary terms has been derived, unwittingly and unintentionally, from association with the intrusive ruling power. Furthermore, the individual in seeking to influence the local situation has been much too much the child of his home community to respond fully to the indigenous values and traditions. The Church has something fundamental to contribute to dealing with the difficulties and to responding to the opportunities of the process of rapid change from rural to urban living. And possibly the best way in which I can draw your attention to that contribution is to end my remarks by commending to you for your thoughtful consideration the report of the ecumenical study conference held last year at Thessalonica by the World Council of Churches, and recently published under the title, *Dilemmas and Opportunities: Christian Action in Rapid Social Change.*